THE ACHIEVEMENT GAP IN U.S. EDUCATION

Canaries in the Mine

Mano Singham

Rowman & Littlefield Education
Lanham, Maryland • Toronto • Oxford
2005

Published in the United States of America
by Rowman & Littlefield Education
An imprint of The Rowman & Littlefield Publishing Group, Inc.
4501 Forbes Boulevard, Suite 200, Lanham, Maryland 20706
www.rowmaneducation.com

PO Box 317
Oxford
OX2 9RU, UK

British Library Cataloguing in Publication Information Available

Library of Congress Cataloging-in-Publication Data
Singham, Mano.
    The achievement gap in U.S. education : canaries in the mine / Mano
Singham.
        p. cm.
    Includes bibliographical references and index.
    ISBN 1-57886-217-5 (pbk. : alk. paper)
    1. Educational equalization—United States. 2. Academic
achievement—United States. I. Title: Achievement gap in US education.
II. Title.
LC213.2.S56 2005
379.2'6—dc22

                                                    2004026788

⊗™ The paper used in this publication meets the minimum requirements of
American National Standard for Information Sciences—Permanence of Paper
for Printed Library Materials, ANSI/NISO Z39.48-1992.
Manufactured in the United States of America.

To Shermila, Dashi, and Ashali

CONTENTS

ACKNOWLEDGMENTS

Some of the material in this book has appeared before in *Phi Delta Kappan* magazine in the articles "Race and Intelligence: What Are the Issues?" (December 1995, p. 271), "The Canary in the Mine: Closing the Achievement Gap between Black and White Students" (September 1998, p. 8), and "The Achievement Gap: Myths and Reality" (April 2003, p. 586). They are used here with permission.

INTRODUCTION

There are a lot of books published each year. To add to that number requires a good reason, one that goes beyond the usual culprits of author vanity and career advancement. Each book has to answer the question: Why was this book written? This is particularly difficult to answer in the exhaustively studied field of education for which there is vast and ever-growing literature. The important subfield dealing with the achievement gap between different ethnic groups in the United States is also a widely discussed topic because many people recognize it as a problem that is long-standing and serious and has major consequences. But despite decades of study and efforts at resolving this dilemma, we have progressed very little toward finding a solution. There is no magic bullet because no single reason or collection of reasons can be fingered as the cause. This failure is enormously frustrating for everyone involved. Why is this particular problem so intractable?

Part of the reason is that any research on human beings is bedeviled by the enormous complexity of the subject matter. I come from the world of physics, in which tightly controlled experimentation is possible because it deals with inanimate objects that behave with predictable regularity, so that if you set up the same initial conditions, you end up with the same result. But even in that orderly area of research, arriving at definite conclusions about the cause of any phenomenon is difficult. In the field of medicine, which deals with mostly the physical aspects of human beings, the causes of diseases are hard to diagnose and treat because human beings are complex organisms.

The situation is vastly more complicated in education since we cannot completely specify the conditions under which we operate. Education and learning are ultimately reflected in changes in the brain, and this is even harder to deal with since something that takes place within the brain is largely hidden from us, notwithstanding the huge advances that have been made recently in brain-scanning technology. Learning is a mysterious and complex process. There is not even a universally accepted definition of what learning is.

We have made some progress in understanding the biological nature of learning. Recent books such as *How People Learn*[1] and *The Art of Changing the Brain*[2] have given us fresh insights into the changes that take place in the brain when learning occurs and how those insights can guide us in becoming more effective teachers. But there are still a lot of major unanswered questions in learning and education, and undoubtedly one of these questions is the cause of the educational achievement gap and what should be done to erase it. As one wades through the vast research literature on this topic, one can find support for almost any thesis that purports to identify the cause of the problem, and one can find evidence for almost any suggestion that claims to be the solution.

Faced with that situation, one can write a book that is of the "on the one hand, on the other hand" variety, which gives arguments for and against each position. The aim of this kind of approach is to attempt to remove the biasing filters through which people view data, to try to see the world "objectively," as it purportedly is, unencumbered by prejudices. But can this really be done? One does not have to be a postmodernist philosopher to suspect that trying to arrive at an unbiased view is enormously difficult, perhaps even impossible, especially with such a highly charged, politically sensitive issue like the achievement gap.

The alternative approach is to write with an attitude. By this I mean that instead of trying to remove all the biasing filters, one can try and see if there is an underlying structure to the problem or patterns in the data. In other words, one tries to find that filter that provides a plausible explanation of the problem and promises a strategy for action that is practicable. In this approach, one tries to make explicit the filters through which one views the world, and the reader is invited to accept or reject the resulting picture that comes into view. Plausibility, not proof, has to be the goal of such an endeavor.

This book is of the latter kind. I have tried to look at the problem of the achievement gap in the context of larger political realities. I argue that while the problem of the achievement gap is quite concrete and localized, its causes lie embedded in a larger problem, and it is only by tackling the larger problem that we can hope to solve the specific problem. That larger problem is that we are not doing a good job of teaching *in general*, and the size of the achievement gap should be viewed as a measure of our failure to teach *all* students, not just the currently underachieving ones. In other words, the achievement gap is a by-product of a systemic failure to implement teaching practices that create the conditions for real learning to occur for *all* students.

Much of the data examined in this book deals with black–white comparisons, and less so with the sizeable Hispanic community. This is not because the issue of Hispanic-student underachievement is any less important. It is because more data on black–white differences exist. Also, as will become clear, the main aim of this book is to emphasize the need to shift attention *away* from the minority-community performance, to argue that the problems in education may not lie primarily with them. I use the black–white comparisons mainly as a paradigm for the more general problem of differences in performance based on ethnicity or gender.

This book argues that the way to understand the black–white achievement gap is to not focus exclusively on what is happening in the black community but to look at what is happening with the educational system as a whole. Can I prove that this is the correct way to view the problem? No. Applying a filter to view a problem results in certain features of the problem springing to the foreground and thereby being emphasized, while the rest become part of the background. One can always find alternative filters through which to view the problem, resulting in a different foreground/background separation. It is like viewing the night sky using ultraviolet wavelength or radio wavelength sensitive telescopes. One then sees cosmic patterns that are not visible using the naked eye. The resulting pictures are very different. Which of the three patterns is the "true" picture of the night sky? None of them. Each one highlights some features at the expense of others. They each serve different purposes and provide different insights.

Given this choice of what filters one can use, one is faced with the quandary of selecting the most appropriate one. The only test is whether the picture that comes into view through the filter is plausible and whether the strategies for its solution are workable and, more importantly, just and equitable for all concerned. The filter I use to view the achievement-gap problem suggests strategies for its solution that take into account some of the most sophisticated knowledge about learning theory, and that is its main advantage. The suggested solutions also have the advantage that *all* people interested in improving education can support them and will benefit from them. Many of the solutions to the achievement-gap problem advocated in the past are not implemented because they focus on actions directed at the minority community alone, and, given the political climate in which we live, such targeted allocations of resources and effort tend to lack the broad-based political support necessary for successful implementation.

Understanding the main argument of this book requires a delicate balancing act, and I want to make very explicit what the argument is and what it is not. While acknowledging that there are many factors influencing black-student underachievement, the book argues that treating current white-student performance as being at acceptable levels and trying to raise black-student achievement levels to those of white students is not going to be an effective strategy. This book argues that what we actually have are two levels of underachievement. White students underachieve, and black students underachieve even more. So closing the gap in the conventional sense by bringing black-student achievement up to the level of white students merely results in equal levels of underachievement, hardly a noble goal. The achievement gap we should be focusing on is the gap between where students are and where they *should* be. This is a far more challenging problem, mainly because it requires shaking the white community out of a sense of complacency that things are fine in their sector of the educational world.

Having said that, I want to caution those critics of public education who wish to see its role reduced (or even disappear) that they will get no support from me. Such people tend to view broad critiques of education as supporting their view that public education has failed completely and should be replaced by other systems based on market models. Those who hope to find comfort and support in this book for measures to undermine public education and transfer its resources to private and parochial schools by cutting funding to public schools and using vouchers to divert funds away from them will be disappointed.

I am a firm believer in the value of free, public education as a great institution. I also happen to view the education given to students in private and parochial schools, even very elite ones, not as models of what constitutes good education, but as suffering from the same deficiencies as public schools. What will be argued in this book is that there is a fundamental problem with the way we teach all students, indeed with the way we view education itself.

In researching and writing about the topic of the achievement gap, I have found it impossible to treat the subject dispassionately. The social and historical injustices that cause the gap, and the further injustices that result from the gap, are so serious and have such devastating consequences for so many children and young adults that one cannot help but feel anger that this state of affairs has been allowed to continue for so long.

This book is written with not only anger but also sadness, sadness that one of the purest forms of enjoyment anyone can have, namely learning, has become for our students merely a chore. If one were to try to identify the one pleasure in life that has the least negatives associated with it, learning must surely rank high. After all, what can be more exciting than finding out something that one did not know before, making sense of ideas and phenomena that had hitherto been puzzling? And yet, for the vast majority of students today (and in days gone by), learning is viewed as drudgery, something they have to be forced to do. For so many teachers and students and school administrators, the school day is not approached with eager anticipation at the prospect of another day of adventure in acquiring new knowledge, but instead as something to be gotten through, to be endured until the weekend, the holiday breaks, the summer vacations, and finally graduation (for students) or retirement (for teachers) arrives and they can go on to do something they really like.

Of course people are learning all the time in their daily lives, and they do get enjoyment from it. It is impossible to experience life without learning from it. But in the classroom and schoolhouse, the places where one would think people would get the most enjoyment from learning because of the focused attention on it and the ready access to learning materials, people, and other resources that can facilitate the learning process, that sense of enjoyment seems to disappear to be replaced by a numbing sense of routine administered in an atmosphere of coercion.

This book is also written in hope. I don't believe that the desire to learn and the enjoyment that comes from it can ever be completely eliminated in anyone. Even in the bleakest surroundings, spontaneous and joyous learning can and still does break through. It is true that these feelings can be dampened and may remain dormant for long periods of time. It is also possible that we can forget what learning can truly be like and get accustomed to its fake substitutes, the ones that are measured by our current regimen of tests and grades and certificates. But even this cannot completely kill the intrinsic love of learning that lies deep within all of us.

This book argues that the reason we have achievement gaps is because of the underlying philosophy of the educational system and identifies the main source of the problem as lying with the quality of teaching available to students. But, and this is extremely important to appreciate, this is by no means a "blame the teachers" book. I have met many teachers who care passionately about teaching and spend their own money to provide supplies for their students that their school districts cannot or will not. I have also met many teachers who have an impressive command of the subject matter they are required to teach and an awareness of the standards they need to meet. And I have met teachers who have superb technical skills in the many variants of active-learning methods. And there are some teachers who have an intuitive sense of what motivates students to want to learn.

What is rare, however, is to find all these qualities in a *single* teacher. But when they are, these teachers achieve remarkable results. Not only does the achievement gap decrease dramatically, but the performance of *all* students improves. In other words, we achieve both increased overall quality and increased equity.

Such exceptional teachers are not born this way; they become so, due to a variety of mostly fortuitous circumstances. Research indicates that it takes about 10 years of sustained professional development to turn even a knowledgeable, talented, and enthusiastic novice teacher into the kind of seasoned professional who can make a real difference in the learning of all students. This is true for both K–12 and college teachers. But beginning teachers often are not given this kind of support but instead are simply thrust into classrooms and left to fend for themselves. Or they get the kind of ad hoc, scattershot, one-day workshops that pass for professional development in most school districts. In fact, teaching is perhaps unique among professions in the way it hires trained people and, once they are on board, fails to provide them with the ongoing opportunities to develop and advance their skills, to enable them to reach that higher level that makes them self-developing professionals. This book calls for such professional-development programs to be implemented in all school districts as part of their routine operations.

This book also argues that these actions have to be aimed at the whole body of teachers, not just at those who are teaching the lower-achieving students. This is important because it is a sad truth that programs aimed at only poor and underserved communities lack the long-term political and financial support needed to make them part of the regular structure.

When I look back on my own career in teaching, the main regret I have lies with all the students I taught before I personally rediscovered the joy of learning. For all those years, I underestimated the desire of my students to learn for its own sake, despite the many oblique clues they gave me that I was wrong. I had become so steeped in the popular view that students are not like us teachers when we were students and view schooling as merely a vehicle to get credentials that I ended up believing it too. As a result, I taught in a coercive and authoritarian way, as if students had to be forced to learn.

It was not easy to break free of that mind-set. I have to thank my students for making me realize that the desire to learn is widespread and deep but that both teachers and students cannot see this because it is covered by a heavy shroud of dense, boring, and irrelevant curricula; pedantic and unimaginative teaching; testing mania run rampant; and rigid, conformist, and authoritarian educational structures.

Finally, this book is a call to action. I know that I am not alone, that there are many other people out there who share my belief that the desire to learn is not extinguished in our students, but only dormant. I hope they find the ideas and strategies within these pages useful in fanning those embers. At its heart, this book is an appeal to all those who love learning for its own sake to join together and help make that feeling universal.

NOTES

1. John D. Bransford, Ann L. Brown, and Rodney R. Cocking, eds., *How People Learn* (Washington, DC: National Academy Press, 1999).

2. James E. Zull, *The Art of Changing the Brain* (Sterling, VA: Stylus Publishing, 2002).

2

EDUCATION IN THE BROAD POLITICAL CONTEXT

All men by nature desire to know.

So says Aristotle in the first line of his *Metaphysics*, articulating a sentiment that should warm the hearts of all teachers. What could be more delightful for any teacher than the prospect of facing a sea of faces eager to feast on the knowledge that is laid before them. And yet nearly all modern educational practices seem to be based on the contrary view, that students resist learning at all costs and have to be threatened, bribed, wheedled, and cajoled into acquiring knowledge. Our entire structure of grades, certification, attendance, and graduation requirements are built on the premise that if left to themselves students would do anything else other than learn. So was the great philosopher Aristotle wrong? Or did he mean something different?

If Aristotle's aphorism is correct, then the present lack of enthusiasm for school is a measure of how far removed our schools have become from real knowing and how dramatic has become the separation between true learning and the ability to perform well on tests.

Learning is natural. We do it all the time, consciously and unconsciously. It is as automatic as breathing. Young children are such powerful learners that in many multilingual societies they become fluent in several languages with little formal guidance, even before entering school. This is despite the fact that learning a language is a highly complex cognitive process, which for most adults presents an enormously difficult challenge. In the period of revolutionary America and the early years after independence, almost the entire nonslave population could read, despite little formal schooling. And this universal literacy was attained while they were learning to read difficult books by authors like James Fenimore Cooper and the political pamphlets of Thomas Paine and others.[1]

In his book *The Underground History of American Education*, John Taylor Gatto points out that in the 1840 census, only one citizen out of 579 was considered illiterate, despite the fact that the standard of literacy was much higher than it is now. But by the year 2000, surveys by NAEP (National Assessments of Educational Progress, popularly referred to as "the nation's report card") and NALS (National Adult Literacy Survey) indicated that 40 percent of blacks and 17 percent of whites cannot read at all.[2] How can it be that in modern America, with its universal schooling, teaching people to read has come to be perceived as this enormously difficult challenge, employing numerous experts and schemes and resources, while the results are worse than they were 200 years ago? Answering that question is an important part of understanding the causes of the achievement gap.

But it is not only with language that children demonstrate their prodigious talent for spontaneous learning. From the time children are born, they are figuring out how the world works and how they can navigate their way through it. Long before they even get to school, and without any formal effort at instruction, little children have developed complex theories about the world. These theories are remarkably effective in enabling children to deal with the situations they encounter in everyday life. Adults may consider some of these beliefs (for example, the common childhood view that the world is flat) to be naïve or even completely wrong, but the theories are effective in that they enable the child to live and function efficiently.

In fact, it is precisely because these beliefs have kernels of truth (the world, for almost all intents and purposes, can justifiably be treated as flat for the kinds of distances that children experience) that they are so robust and resistant to change by the efforts of teachers. As we will see later, this vast and rich storehouse of prior knowledge that children acquire in their daily lives can, if understood, respected, and used correctly by teachers, be the greatest asset in student learning, but if ignored or belittled (which, alas, is the more common occurrence) it can render futile the efforts of even the most conscientious teacher.

Learning occurs naturally because it also provides pleasure. The quiet enjoyment that comes with acquiring new knowledge (as simple as learning a new word), understanding something that was previously puzzling (why the sky is blue or the reasons for the seasons, for example), mastering something on one's own (say a game or a musical instrument), or figuring out how to do something well (cultivating a garden, creating a new recipe, fixing a problem with your car, hitting or throwing a ball accurately) is hard to describe, but is very real nonetheless. It is this pleasure that causes us to want to learn more.

So Aristotle's assumption about the natural human thirst for knowledge is correct when describing either spontaneous learning or the learning of something that the learner chooses to do in his or her own way. But this does not accurately describe what goes on in schools. The educational system tries to get students to learn material that they usually do not find relevant or interesting, and at a time, place, and pace, and in a sequence and style, that are not of the students' own choosing. It should not be surprising that Aristotle's optimism proves unwarranted under these adverse circumstances and that when we look at the performance of students placed in these very institutions (our schools and colleges) that are supposed to enhance learning, the results are disappointing. Teachers in the K–12 sector find it a struggle to teach even the basic elements of reading, writing, and mathematics. College faculty complain of students who are not interested in the subject matter of their courses but instead see themselves as customers who are merely purchasing a certificate that leads to employment. Complaints abound everywhere about student apathy and lack of interest, or even downright hostility to learning.

To be fair, such complaints are not universal. There are pockets of satisfaction. Teachers of students in "gifted" programs or in advanced and accelerated tracks tend not to complain of these problems, which make these teaching assignments much sought after. But teachers of "ordinary" students have no such luck. As a result, some people have concluded that real learning is something only a few have a capacity and taste for and that we should focus our more earnest teaching efforts on identifying, selecting, and nurturing this small group of elite students who seem to have a natural affinity for learning and can benefit from it. But under close examination, even this more limited expectation seems unwarranted.

For instance, in December 2001, the *Washington Post* had a story about "Jeff," identified as one of these gifted students. He was a high-achieving high school senior in suburban Washington who suddenly dropped out of his advanced-placement (AP) class on government and enrolled in an "easier" class. The reason for this abrupt switch? He had just received notice that he had been accepted to the University of Pennsylvania under its early-acceptance program. Under these programs, students who have a clear preference about where they want to go to college and are reasonably confident of their chances are encouraged to apply for early acceptance. The students are informed of the university's decision in December of their senior year, much earlier than the usual April decision time, and their acceptance will not be subsequently withdrawn unless under exceptional circumstances.

Since the University of Pennsylvania does not allow AP credit for government to replace any part of its own internal course requirements, the high school AP class he was enrolled in suddenly became "useless" (at least in Jeff's eyes), and he did not see any point in pursuing it. The *Post* article used this story to highlight a scenario that is being repeated all over the country. Apparently more and more high-achieving students, those members of the academic elite who are in the most advanced tracks, are using their early acceptances from colleges to opt out of the very kinds of high school courses that enabled them to gain admission to those same elite universities in the first place. This is causing serious concern and calls for action.

What immediately struck me about the story was how the author of the article, and the school authorities interviewed for it, viewed the situation. The problem was perceived as essentially a *bureaucratic* one: How can we prevent more students from behaving like Jeff and switching out of these advanced classes? How can we make sure that early acceptance does not become the cause of lowered high school academic ambition? Various administrative strategies were proposed. Some colleges were going to limit the number of students they accept early, thus lowering the number of potential "dropouts." Also, some high school teachers and counselors are reportedly telling their students not to apply for early admission at all so they will not have the option of dropping courses early.

To my mind, the really interesting question is why so-called gifted students are dropping advanced courses the first chance they get. It is no great mystery, though the article does not pursue the issue. Jeff himself makes no secret of his own reasons. He disliked the teacher and "really didn't like the course at all." He was just doing it because it looked good on college application forms. It is quite plausible that this is the reason that drives other students to take the same action. So it is possible to argue that the real problem highlighted by Jeff's story is an *educational* one: What is it about these courses that so alienate students? And the real strategy that should be worked on is how to design courses that students will *want* to take for their own sake, without having to be induced by external rewards or coerced by bureaucratic restrictions.

In fact, this story highlights a mind-set that is endemic in our schools and colleges. Learning is rarely presented to students as something that is worth doing *for its own sake*. Its main function is perceived to be to prepare students for something else. So the purpose of a college education is to prepare students for graduate school or for careers, high school is to prepare for college or for work, and middle school is to learn material that is presumably useful in high school. Further down the chain, elementary school is seen as preparing children for middle school, and preschool programs are seen as necessary to get students ready for school. This dismal view of education is not a recent development but has a venerable history. In the 1922 novel *Babbitt* by Sinclair Lewis, for example, the title character responds impatiently to his high-school-age son who cannot understand why he is made to learn all the useless stuff in school. Babbitt tells him, "I'll tell you why you have to study Shakespeare and those. It's because they're required for college entrance, and that's all there is to it!"[3]

In all this preparatory work for some amorphous future benefit, when do students get the chance to learn something just because it is interesting? Or because it piques their curiosity? Or because it captures their imagination? Sadly, for many students the answer is never.

The strange thing is that many people who seem to advocate the prevailing model of education as medicine ("Take it; it may taste bad now,

but it's good for you and you'll feel better later") are the very people who
share Aristotle's secret: *Learning is really enjoyable*. All of us in the field
of education get immense satisfaction from learning all kinds of things.
There is great pleasure to be derived from seeing something one did not
see before, in mastering something that seems initially formidable, in
finding subtleties in the seemingly obvious, and in making connections
between ideas that seem distinct. These are the great emotional rewards
for a life spent in learning and education.

The late physicist Richard Feynman had such a zest for learning and
spoke about the deep sense of satisfaction he felt when he realized that
he had, during the course of his research, discovered something that no
one else seemed to know. He said it was hard to describe the feeling of
being in sole possession of some new piece of knowledge prior to publishing it and making it more widely known. But that sense of satisfaction is not reserved just for researchers at the frontiers of knowledge. It
can be felt even if the knowledge gained is not totally new. All that is
necessary is that it be novel for us, the learner. So why don't our students
experience this feeling? Why do we think our students won't want to
learn unless they are coerced and bribed into doing it? Do we think our
students are somehow different from us? Do we think they do not, and
perhaps *cannot*, share in our own love of learning?

That is not what the students who are supposedly slacking because of
early admission seem to think. According to the *Washington Post* article,
they "not only want a chance to choose intriguing courses that might not
impress colleges, but they also feel they are entitled to a break after
years of academic pressure." In other words, after about a dozen years
on the education treadmill, with its philosophy of "you must learn this
now because you will need it later and bad things will happen to you
otherwise," they are looking for a chance to do something just because
it intrigues them, and to do it in a relaxed atmosphere. This slender evidence that the spirit of learning has not been totally extinguished in
students (despite our determined efforts) should be viewed as a hopeful
sign that Aristotle was right. But it is actually being deplored, as if it is
reprehensible that students should desire a choice in what they learn
and how they learn it.

One might be tempted to dismiss the whole *Washington Post* article as
just reflecting the whining of already pampered elites. After all, we are

talking about high-achieving suburban students, teachers, and administrators who are complaining about the effects of admission policies of elite colleges. But the pernicious effect of this "education as medicine" philosophy pervades the school system at all levels. And I will argue that it provides an important clue as to how we should deal with the serious and widespread problem of the educational achievement gap.

Take the case of mathematics. The Cleveland School District (which has about two-thirds black and Hispanic students) regularly reports deplorable results in Ohio's statewide proficiency tests. The tests cover reading, writing, social studies, science, and mathematics, and in order to graduate from high school, students must pass tests in all these subjects. The tests are currently pitched at the eighth-grade knowledge level, yet large numbers of high school *seniors* in Cleveland do not graduate, largely because they have not passed the mathematics portion of the test. Typically only about 20 percent of Cleveland's students pass the mathematics test on their first attempt.[4] This low result occurs despite students' being repeatedly told by parents, teachers, community leaders, newspapers, and other influential authorities how important mathematics is to their futures and how useful it will be to them. Why is the message not getting through?

Perhaps it is because the fundamental appeal of mathematics does not lie in its usefulness. I do not know a single mathematician who decided to go into mathematics primarily because it was going to be useful to him or her. The fact that they are able to do their tax returns more accurately, calculate the best return on their investments, or determine whether they should buy outright or finance their new car, plays no role in their decision to study the subject. Some, like the mathematician G. H. Hardy, actually point to the *uselessness* of so-called pure mathematics as one of its most appealing features![5]

Of course mathematics (and science and history and literature and almost any other academic discipline you care to name) is useful in one way or another. That is not the point here. The point is that this is not the prime reason that scholars choose to devote their lives to the subject. They delve deeply into their chosen discipline because, for some reason or other, they want to know more about it. Something about the subject intrigued them. Mathematicians are glad their subject is useful, because then it provides them with a livelihood, and they do not want to feel like parasites on society. But if mathematics *for its own sake* had not intrigued them, they would not have chosen to do it.

Why should the teaching of *any subject* at *any level* not have that same goal: to give students a sense of why people devote their whole lives to learning more about it? The only reason not to teach this way is if we believe that most students are not like us, that they cannot appreciate the intrinsic appeal of a subject, and that the only reason for studying it is because of extrinsic rewards such as its future utility, either to get a job, a high school diploma, or college admission.

Alfie Kohn, in his book *Punished by Rewards*,[6] gives evidence that such bribes and rewards, rather than enhancing the desire to learn, actually act as *inhibitors* to learning. Their net effect is to encourage those who value the rewards to do just enough to get them, and no more. So Jeff's behavior in dropping his AP government class is perfectly rational and consistent. After all, he took AP courses to improve his chances of getting into the college of his choice, and once he had achieved this goal, he did not take any more. The joy of learning played no role in the process. Jeff responded exactly as we trained him to do.

But what about those students for whom such extrinsic rewards either have no value or are seen as unattainable? This is the case for many students in urban poverty centers such as Cleveland. For them, college is seen as an unrealistic dream, and graduating from high school does not seem to promise a life that is much different compared with dropping out. Indeed, for some of the children in these schools, "death at an early age" (actual physical death in addition to the intellectual death starkly profiled by Jonathan Kozol in the book of that name[7]) is not as unthinkable as it is for the rest of us.

I remember vividly a discussion with sixth-grade students in an East Cleveland elementary school. (East Cleveland is a city that is very poor and almost 100 percent black.) The young children spoke about their lives, the drug dealing and the shootings in their neighborhoods. What was remarkable and sad was how matter-of-fact their attitude was toward disturbing issues of life and death, issues that young children from more affluent homes rarely have to contend with. It should not be surprising that the "education as medicine" philosophy of teaching is not as effective with these students in elevating their performance as it is with students for whom college and white-collar careers are realistic expectations for their future.

It is absurd to think that high school seniors in Cleveland cannot pass an eighth-grade mathematics test because of any intrinsic inability, or that the reason they fail is because they lack some set of skills they can be induced to acquire by using appropriate bribes, or that they are unaware of the usefulness of mathematics for many careers. I believe that if they *wanted* to, these students could easily acquire the necessary knowledge and tools to pass the tests. It has to be the case that, for whatever reason, they have decided that these tests serve no meaningful purpose, and they see no point in expending any serious effort to pass them. Low academic achievement (at least as measured by these formal assessment measures) flows inexorably from that premise.

The only reason such students will devote the time and effort to learn something, anything, in depth (and there is no doubt that it does take considerable effort to achieve in-depth understanding and knowledge) is because it is more interesting to do so than the alternatives available to them. After all, that is why *we* choose to spend our time reading and learning. Shouldn't we devote our efforts to finding ways to give students at all grade levels the same sense of wonder that we have about our chosen subjects?

This is not going to be easy. Part of the problem is that many misconceptions surround the question of what makes for effective learning. The first misconception that must be overcome is the one that emphasizes entertainment as an important part of learning. Some people note that students are easily induced to spend many hours watching TV and films or playing video games, and they recommend using some of this glitz to enthuse students. But learning is not entertainment. While real learning can be "entertaining" (in the sense that time passes rapidly when we are deeply engrossed and actively engaged in the learning process), entertainment by itself does not lead to learning. We should not fall into the trap of trying to impress or amuse students with theatricality or of going down the path of teacher as entertainer and students as enthralled observers. These strategies, like watching television, produce only short-term interest and leave no lasting learning imprint.

Other misconceptions about learning (popularized in countless films and television programs) are that it takes a charismatic teacher to inspire students or that the teacher's own enthusiasm for the subject can generate interest in students. Neither of these assumptions is valid. Of course teacher personality is important, and it is better to have a teacher who is enthusiastic about her subject than one who is not, but these qualities *by themselves* are not sufficient to create an interest in learning in students. Too much teacher charisma and dynamism can also have the unwanted side effect of encouraging students to be more passive and to act like audience members rather than like engaged participants. Students may be deceived into thinking that learning is easy because the teacher makes it seem so.

The real enjoyment of learning comes when students experience *for themselves* the exhilaration of putting ideas together, of working something out for themselves, or of creating something new in their own minds. Once students experience the real enjoyment and challenge of learning something meaningful and achieve some success at it, they are more likely to pursue it for its own sake. And once they become addicted to this experience (and I use the word "addicted" deliberately, because enjoyable learning is habit-forming), there is little they cannot achieve. Getting them to that point is the real challenge of teaching.

We need to look at those things that actually influence how students view learning and at what we can do to create in classrooms those conditions that create a positive view of it. The evidence suggests that if we can create the conditions for real learning to occur *for all students*, the achievement gap narrows and even disappears. In other words, reducing or removing the educational gap may require us to shift our focus away from looking exclusively at minority performance, paradoxical as that may seem.

Making this case is not going to be easy, for several reasons. One is that research on education is inherently messy. In social sciences research, one cannot hope for the tightly controlled experimental conditions of the natural sciences. But even allowing for that, trying to isolate the factors that influence learning is notoriously difficult. There are so many confounding variables that it is not easy to arrive at unambiguous conclusions about what works and what does not work in education.

For example, measuring achievement is a complicated business. What constitutes learning? Are we interested in learning or in students' acquiring certain specific skills (the two things are not synonymous)?

What instruments should be used to measure achievement? How valid are they?

Measuring the effectiveness of any educational intervention is also difficult. How general are the results? How does one evaluate the contributions of other factors that may have swayed the outcome?

Furthermore, a huge amount and variety of educational achievement data exist on a wide range of samples. These data spring from a range of disciplines (sociology, psychology, anthropology, statistics, education theory, and cognitive sciences), each using different methodologies and research protocols and applied to different age groups of learners. In this wealth of data, it is always possible to find support for (and counterarguments against) almost any proposition about what should be done about education. So there is an element of taste and judgment that goes into the selection of data to buttress any argument, and this immediately lays one open to the charge of bias or of using political criteria in drawing one's conclusions.

Discussions on problems in education are also plagued by an overemphasis on personal experiences. There is no intrinsic harm in using one's own experiences as the starting point for understanding the problems of education. The reader will find that this book is peppered with examples based on my own experiences. It would be hard for me to justify any recommendation that did not ring true based on my own involvement with teaching students (assuming I have analyzed these events carefully), and I would expect this to be the same for anyone else. As I stated before and will argue again later, such prior knowledge and experience is the foundation of any learning and has to be accommodated. The problem is with people who never get beyond the purely personal and idiosyncratic, who see no need to also think of the problem in more general terms and in light of scholarship.

For example, my own local newspaper has as one of its regular columnists someone who constantly refers to the teachers of his own youth as exemplars. When the usually dismal results of statewide proficiency tests are periodically reported, this person will rail at the current state of education and pronounce that the reason is the lack of discipline in schools and the mollycoddling of students, coupled with newfangled and untested teaching ideas from ivory-tower education academics. He will fondly recall the teachers of his own youth who would rap him on the knuckles when he did not do his homework or learn the multiplication tables. And, by golly, he learned, which is how he became the successful man he is today. He "took his medicine," and he became well.

Implicit in this criticism is the idea that what is needed now is more of the firm yet well-intentioned authoritarianism of the teachers he had in the past. But while such critics use their own success to argue for the return of teacher qualities they perceive as having been effective, they rarely reflect (at least in public) on whether those teachers were as successful as they assume. For example, how many of their student peers also became "successful," accepting for the moment this narrow definition of success? Were the disciplinarian teachers more successful than the teachers of today in educating a larger number of students? Were they even more successful than their contemporaries who were not so stern? Such general questions are rarely posed. The writer's own professional success is deemed sufficient to make sweeping conclusions, rather than as a starting point for a more thorough investigation and analysis.

In fact, one of the hidden biases of education is that the people who are now in a position to influence the system are the very people, possibly a small minority, who were successful in the existing system. There is no doubt they feel convinced that the system worked for them, but such people may have a distorted view of the effectiveness of the system they grew up in. We need to look more closely to see if it worked well for everybody, or for at least a significant portion.

Which brings us to one of the biggest obstacles to looking dispassionately at education. Education is one of the most politically charged of all fields, especially in the United States. It generates intense passions, it is the target of ideologues of all political persuasions, it is viewed with suspicion as the purveyor of hidden agendas, and it is the most scrutinized. Even the most commonplace assumptions are challenged; thus it is almost impossible to start from a common and agreed-upon framework. For example, most people in the field of education would argue that teaching students to learn how to think critically is an unexceptionable goal that would garner universal support. But in my local newspaper, an op-ed column that made this assumption drew a sharp reader response in the form of a letter to the editor. The letter writer argued that even this seemingly trite observation about the value of teaching students to think was in actuality subversive nonsense and that what students really need is a "strong base" of "traditional morality."

Education is also, not coincidentally, a field in which there is still some resemblance of local control, with locally elected school boards having some degree of say in what the children of that area are taught and how they should be taught. In general, this is a good thing. To have people care about something, know something about it, and have some degree of say in how it is run forms the foundation of democracy. But it does create a problem in that you can have a cacophony of voices, each trying to drown the other rather than see the other's point of view. At the two extremes of this debate are the critics and defenders of public education.

In an era when the goal of freely accessible universal health care is seen as politically unfeasible, when Medicare and Medicaid risk being dismantled, when even social security is under siege and threatened with being changed from a collective responsibility to a private system, it should not be surprising that public schooling has also been under attack. After all, the public schools are, at least in principle, one of the last sources of social mobility and egalitarian thinking. It is one of the few avenues by which poor parents can hope for a better future for their children.

There is no question that the political climate that currently exists is hostile to the notion of universal and freely accessible public services. The notion that everyone should have equal and unfettered access to free high-quality education is being challenged. There is strong pressure to "privatize" education, to take public funds and use them to send children to private schools through mechanisms such as vouchers.

This drive to privatize schools is partly driven by those who believe, on ideological grounds, that market forces should permeate all aspects of our lives and that having purely taxpayer-funded schools is wrong. It is also aided by those who dislike the avowedly secular nature of public schooling and see it as the incubator of the dreaded "secular humanism" philosophy that they feel is responsible for the nation's alleged moral degeneracy. Such people (like the letter writer quoted above) would like to see religious and moral instruction introduced in education. Such people want to create the public equivalent of parochial schools.

But the privatization drive is also motivated by more mercenary concerns. K–12 education is an over $400 billion not-for-profit enterprise, largely controlled by publicly elected bodies. There is a huge amount of money to be made if even a small fraction of that budget can be converted to private profit, and this has attracted the attention of the entrepreneurial class. Hence we see the advent of private companies that seek to take over public schools and run them as for-profit ventures.

All these groups have a vested interest in arguing that public schools have failed hopelessly and are beyond repair, and that the only solution is to take them out of the public's hands and place them in private ones.

The defenders of public education have pointed out that such broad-brush criticisms of public education are unwarranted and misleading. Researcher Gerald Bracey, in his books[8] and his regular monthly column in *Phi Delta Kappan* magazine, has long been pointing out that the mass media has abetted these efforts at undermining confidence in public schools by taking an asymmetric approach to coverage of education. Reporters tend to trumpet any indications of failure in the educational system while ignoring or downplaying any signs of success. It seems they delight in stories showing that public schools are perilously close to disaster, that the nation's future is at risk, and that students today are abysmally ignorant. Any economic downturn is promptly blamed on the fact that schools are not producing the kinds of workers with high-tech skills that are needed to make the U.S. economy competitive.

What is curious is that these ominous warnings have been around for many decades (the most famous doomsday Department of Education report, *A Nation at Risk*, was published in 1983), so if these dire predictions had come true, the U.S. economy should right now be in a catastrophic state. The fact that this is not so does not seem to cause puzzlement among these prophets of doom. Also, no one praises the schools when the economy and the stock markets go through their periodic upturns. This curious wallowing in failure lies in stark contrast to the way the media portrays other public institutions (such as the military), where it is the successes that are publicized and the failures that are underreported.

Researchers David Berliner and Bruce Biddle, also defenders of public schools, have noted that when comparing the performance of U.S. schools against those of other nations, the use of average scores hides the fact that the United States is a nation of extremes. Some school districts (usually suburban) compare very well with their international peers, while others (usually urban or rural) do poorly.[9] Bracey and Berliner and Biddle argue that evaluating the performance of schools and students is not simple, and one has to take a nuanced attitude. Rather than view the whole public school system as a failure, one should focus on the poorly performing schools and do what it takes to improve their performance. Bracey also makes the important point that using rankings to evaluate schools internationally is also misleading because sometimes only a few points separate the nations at the top from those in the middle of the pack.

This book takes a different view. I believe the public education system is one of the most valuable vehicles for social justice, social mobility, and democracy, and it would be a horrendous crime to contribute to its demise. Without public schools, people would be trapped in a form of class tyranny even worse than what currently exists, where only rich people would have access to the kind of quality education that would make them even more powerful.

While I agree with Bracey and Berliner and Biddle that one needs to recognize the huge diversity in education in the United States, I also feel that the educational system as a whole has serious problems. But my criticisms of education, as can be seen above from the story of Jeff's disengagement from AP courses, extend to the suburban, parochial, and private schools as well. While many public schools do come out poorly on some measures when compared with private schools or some school systems in other countries, these measures are not the ones that measure real learning. There is no reason to think that private, parochial, or elite suburban public schools have better educational philosophies and practices than the many troubled school districts (usually urban and minority-dominated) that serve as poster children for the alleged failure of public schooling.

I also argue that the existence of the achievement gap is an indicator that there are fundamental problems in the way we educate *all* our children (whether they be in public or private schools), irrespective of race or ethnicity. The widespread use of this flawed and misguided educational philosophy and practice, even when applied uniformly to all students, has a *differential* impact on the performance of different groups and thus exacerbates the achievement gap between black and white students.

It is not going to be easy to convince elite opinion makers of this point of view. Such people tend to feel that the education they personally received (whatever form it took) has been good (after all, they did become "successful") and that the problem lies in how to broaden the reach of such educational measures. To convince such people that they became what they are, not because of, but *despite* the education they received is not going to be an easy sell. For one thing, if my argument is correct, then the question that has to be addressed is how the system has failed in such a widespread and spectacular manner.

When a long-standing and major undertaking (like the education system) fails to produce the results expected of it, the initial assumption is that, while the goals of the system are well intentioned, the system has somehow gone awry because of failures of implementation due to technical reasons. Thus a search is undertaken to identify the factors (such as unstable family structures, poor teacher training, inadequate curricular materials and supplies, etc.) that caused the debacle, and strategies are devised to either overcome them or, if that is not possible, at least compensate for them.

But there is an alternative way of looking at such a situation. Perhaps the system *is* functioning as designed, but the goals of the system are not the noble, publicly articulated ones. In other words, the dismal results we now produce, rather than being unwanted outcomes of a well-intentioned system, are actually successful outcomes of an ill-intentioned system. Perhaps the educational system was designed to produce only a relatively small fraction of successful people destined for higher education. This elite would serve as the ruling and managerial classes to oversee the activities of the rest. The majority are destined to work docilely at the many routine and cognitively low-level tasks required by the modern economy. The educational system also provides the elites with the technical skills and training that enable them to serve as opinion makers who mold and shape public attitudes. The rest remain bewildered by the complexity of modern life and docilely and unquestioningly accept the opinions of "experts" on all the major issues (political, social, economic, and so on) that affect their lives.

This scenario may initially sound far-fetched, the product of a fevered and dark imagination. But I invite the reader to step back and look unflinchingly at the world around her. Is it not true that we have abdicated decision-making power in all the major areas of our lives to an elite group, that we are made to feel that issues important to us are highly complicated, and that we should trust the "experts" (in government, industry, academia, and the media) to make these decisions for us? Aren't we being constantly urged to abdicate our rights of participation in the decision-making processes and to trust the authorities to act on our behalf, except for the occasional act of voting to select from a highly winnowed field of similar candidates? Could such a vast undermining of the democratic ideal happen by chance? I will argue that it is not an accident.

But you do not have to simply take my word for this. The case for this viewpoint is examined in detail in the last chapter, where we look at the question of how we got the educational system we now have. In reality it is a well-documented point of view. The reason it seems so strange and even subversive now is that these ideas are not discussed publicly at the present time. But at one time it was quite brazenly asserted by influential people that the purpose of the educational system should be to produce a large number of docile people who are good at routine and menial tasks and who accept that this is their proper station in life. But this debate on the purpose of education took place so long ago that most people are unaware it ever occurred.[10]

The educational system we now have was created to produce just such a state, and it has been, by this dubious yardstick, highly "successful," although the inherent contradictions of having such an ignoble goal are now becoming manifest. One of the contradictions surfacing is that the drive to create a tiered social structure with an elite educated class and a less-privileged class to work in lower-level occupations has not been equally effective for the different ethnic groups and has thus created a racial achievement gap that threatens to cause unwanted political instability. If the drive to create a mostly docile and unquestioning public had managed to create one that was also ethnicity and gender neutral, this state of affairs may have remained unquestioned for a long time. But the central thesis of this book is that the negative effects of such a bad educational policy are not neutral. It has a differentially negative impact on ethnicity- and gender-based groupings, and it is the ethnic gap that is the main subject of this book, although the gender differential is no less important.

Let me emphasize this point. It is often believed that if we had equal distribution of all educational resources, and that if all students had equal access to these resources, there would be no educational achievement gaps. But I will argue that this is not so, that ensuring equal resources and equal access is not sufficient to close the gap, even though they are necessary and desirable goals for any society that believes in justice and equity. In particular, even if all students had access to the same resources and teachers but were taught badly or were constrained by an educational system that was based on an inferior philosophy of learning, achievement gaps would appear. So the size of the achievement gap is, in some senses, a measure of how well we teach *all* students, a gauge of the overall health of the system. Black students are "canaries in the mine," whose performance tells us something important about the educational atmosphere that we all find ourselves in. The goal of this book is to provide parents, teachers, and educational administrators with guidelines for providing the kinds of educational experiences that will make students want to learn, and thus reduce the gap.

It is important to understand the relationship between access to resources and learning. Periodically one hears claims that increased funding for schools does not lead to increased learning, and some sectors of educational opinion have seized on this to argue against providing increased funding for low-achieving students and schools. Such people argue that it is futile to "throw money at the problem."[11] My statements in the earlier paragraph may be misconstrued as supporting that view. But what I am saying is that increased and equitable funding is not sufficient, by itself, to close the achievement gap, not that it is not necessary or desirable. We need more than equal resources and equal access.

The educational achievement gap between ethnic groups is one of the most important problems that any nation faces. Persistent gaps in achievement and an increasing sense of inequity can lead to huge social problems and even (as in some countries) civil wars. So it is not a problem that should be dealt with with benign neglect in the hope that some general improvement in other social and economic indicators will bring a commensurate improvement in schools. It is a problem that should be addressed directly, with as much deliberation and care as is possible under the circumstances.

In examining the underlying causes of the achievement gap, we will see that the role of the teacher is critical in such discussions. But as I have said earlier, this is not a "blame the teacher" book, although that is a popular theme of many education analyses. I have enormous sympathy for the difficult conditions under which teachers work and the challenges they are called upon to face. They have been placed in an impossible situation where they are continually exhorted to succeed while subjected to conditions designed for them to fail.

But in addition to the analysis, we will look at possible courses of action and see signs of hope that something can be done. There is encouraging news to report. If the analysis showed that only a broad change in socioeconomic conditions could erase the educational achievement gap, we would have little choice but to sit around and wait for that to occur. If the analysis showed that massive resources had to be devoted to the minority community alone to erase the gap, that policy would be unlikely to gain broad-based political support. In these days of fierce competition for public funding, programs aimed at improving the lot of minority groups, however deserving, are under strong pressure for elimination, on the basis that we have supposedly already achieved a "color-blind" stage of society.

But the analysis and course of action proposed here have none of these disadvantages. It is argued that educational interventions, within the current educational framework, can go a long way toward remedying the achievement-gap problem. These interventions are not ethnically targeted, thus enabling them to garner broad-based support and making them politically feasible. I hope that those who support public schools and want to see them flourish will find the suggestions in the subsequent pages useful in transforming the face of education.

NOTES

1. John Taylor Gatto, *The Underground History of American Education* (New York: The Oxford Village Press, 2003), 31.

2. Gatto, *The Underground History*, 53.

3. Sinclair Lewis, *Babbitt* (New York: Signet Books, 1961), 64.

4. Stephen Ohlemacher, "Test Scores Reveal Width of Racial Gap," *The Plain Dealer*, 4 November 2001, A1.

5. G. H. Hardy, *A Mathematician's Apology* (London: Cambridge University Press, 1967).

6. Alfie Kohn, *Punished by Rewards* (Boston: Houghton Mifflin, 1993).

7. Jonathan Kozol, *Death at an Early Age* (Boston: Houghton Mifflin, 1967).

8. Gerald W. Bracey, *The War against America's Public Schools* (Boston: Allyn and Bacon, 2002).

9. David C. Berliner and Bruce J. Biddle, *The Manufactured Crisis* (Reading, MA: Addison-Wesley, 1995).

10. The reader who is particularly intrigued by this point, or quite skeptical, is urged to read the last chapter now for a more in-depth discussion.

11. It is curious that it is only in the context of increased funding for education that the phrase "to throw money," with all its connotations of wanton wastefulness, is invoked. One rarely hears this phrase used by advocates of increased funding for, say, weapons systems or tax breaks and subsidies for big business. Such people also never seem to take the next logical step of their own argument and argue, since money is supposedly not an important factor in achieving a quality education, in favor of *cutting* funding for the wealthy school systems so that those students would also attend poorly funded and bleak schools with inadequately prepared teachers.

3

MYTHS ABOUT THE
ACHIEVEMENT GAP

On June 23, 2003, the U.S. Supreme Court gave landmark rulings on two affirmative-action cases (*Grutter v. Bollinger* and *Gratz v. Bollinger*) that involved admissions policies at the University of Michigan. The key elements of the rulings are summed up in the following Cable News Network report:

WHAT THE RULINGS MEAN

The Supreme Court struck down a point system used by the University of Michigan to give minorities preference in undergraduate admissions. The court, however, approved a separate program used by the University of Michigan's law school that gives race less prominence in the admissions decision-making process.

The Supreme Court left room for the nation's public universities—and by extension other public and private institutions—to seek subtler ways to take race into account than through a point system. Analysts say the rulings mean that race-conscious policies in place that do not use a point system or other narrow system will probably remain in place.[1]

Opponents of affirmative action, who wanted the court to outlaw all consideration of race in admissions, were dismayed. The Manhattan Institute's Abigail Thernstrom, interviewed by Nina Totenberg on NPR's

Morning Edition on Tuesday, June 24, said she was beside herself with rage at the decision. But Thernstrom is also reported as saying that it was now time to abandon the legal fight and move on to addressing the reason for the racial gap in test scores: the inadequate education of minority students in kindergarten to twelfth grade. Thernstrom continues, "There is no excuse for that racial gap in the elementary and secondary school years. We must close it. It is a moral imperative. And it is not rocket science."

In those brief comments, Thernstrom captured all that is right and all that is wrong in discussions about the achievement gap. She is right that the achievement gap is an urgent problem, that solving it is a moral imperative, and that it is time to stop legal actions and focus on eliminating the gap. But the rest of her remarks reiterate some of the common myths that muddy the discussion, and those myths are what this chapter focuses on.

The first myth is that understanding the achievement-gap problem is simple and that formulating the solution is obvious. The simplicity is often highlighted by contrasting it (as Thernstrom does) with the presumably very difficult science of rocketry. As a physicist, I am somewhat familiar with the elements of rocket science, and it is my belief that rocket science is simple compared to understanding and solving problems in education. In physics (and rocket science), systems behave in a repeatable and predictable fashion, since we are dealing with inanimate objects. The fundamental laws of behavior are reasonably well understood, and there is a broad consensus on how problems should be tackled. The relevant variables can be identified and often controlled. It is relatively straightforward to identify what we know and what we don't know. And with the things we don't know, it is also possible to specify what data we need to collect in order to answer important questions.

But education has none of these advantages. It also has some additional disadvantages, one of the main ones being that with rocket science, people approach the subject with caution, recognizing that they may not know enough to pass definitive judgments. But with education, everyone considers himself or herself an expert because everyone has had some experience of schooling, as a child, often as a parent, and sometimes as a teacher. These "experts" see no reason to go beyond memories of their own school years. And this unwillingness to look deeper into the issues and see the problem as subtle, complex, and multifaceted often prevents meaningful discussions of solutions from taking place.

The second myth highlighted by Thernstrom's statement is that the problem lies solely with the inadequate education received by *minority* students. She makes the implicit assumption that white educational achievement is satisfactory, or at least adequate. As mentioned in the previous chapter, this narrow focus may prevent us from seeing deeper causes of the problem. This approach is an example of a more general characteristic of discussions involving any issue that is being analyzed on the basis of how different ethnic groups perform. The issue could be education, crime, suicide, welfare, teen sex and pregnancy, or anything else that is perceived as creating a problem for society. In such analyses, statistics for whites are usually taken as being the natural or acceptable state of society, and the problem to be solved is framed as being how to improve the black statistics until they reach the level of whites.

In the musical *My Fair Lady*, Professor Henry Higgins plaintively sings, "Why can't a woman be more like man?" implying that the problems of gender-based misunderstandings and conflict could be avoided if women just adopted the values and behavior of men. This same spirit underlies the arguments that focus on how to "improve" black performance so that it reaches the level of whites. If only black people would act like whites, there would be no achievement gap.

To look at the problem in this way is to immediately go off in the wrong direction. Such a view obscures the fact that a large fraction of white students are also underachieving and that this problem is deserving of serious attention as well. In addition, focusing on black-student performance alone is deeply offensive to members of the black community because it points the finger of social pathology directly at them. It has to be realized that black people are not as impressed with the virtues of whites as whites are, and see little need to emulate them. After all, the whites were the ones who brought blacks over as slaves and kept them in abject servitude and poverty for generations. Lynchings, beatings, and being set upon by dogs and buffeted by water from fire hoses are all things that are within living memory of black people. Given this history, to ask blacks to adopt white behavior as role models for virtuousness seems presumptuous, to put it mildly. James Baldwin captured this difference in perception when he said in *The Fire Next Time*, "White Americans find it as difficult as white people elsewhere do to divest themselves of the notion that they are in possession of some intrinsic value that black people need or want. . . . There is certainly little enough in the white man's public or private life that one should desire to imitate."[2]

More recently, the authors of the Web journal *The Black Commentator* expressed a similar view even more strongly, saying,

> The starting point of American racism is the assumption that white people and their institutions represent the proper, normative standards against which all other people and institutions are judged. Once the white normative assumption is internalized, a racist worldview flows from it as surely as water to the sea, polluting every social space in its path.[3]

An exclusive focus on black-student achievement alone may obscure the fact that the achievement gap may be due to the problematic way we approach the teaching of all children of *all* ethnicities (including whites), not just minority ones.

The third myth lies in the assumption that the problem is in the education received by black students in the K–12 years. If that could be improved and brought to par, this way of thinking goes, there would be no need for affirmative action. This view is a special case of the belief that black students fall behind because of a lack of specific knowledge or skills at some given time in their progress along the educational track, and it forms the basis of the many remedial programs that seek to bring students up to the "same starting line" (to use a commonly used phrase) as that of whites. Bring them up to speed, the argument goes, and they will maintain that speed. It is rarely questioned as to whether this belief is valid.

It is not so much where students are at any point in their education that is the predictor of future success, but what kinds of learning methods they have used and what learning skills they have acquired up to that point and feel comfortable using. It is quite possible to drill students so that they acquire whatever pieces of knowledge are deemed important at a particular grade level. But if the methods used to teach them this knowledge require mainly low-level cognitive skills (such as rote memory), then the students will lack the kinds of sophisticated learning skills that will enable them to acquire more advanced knowledge quickly and efficiently, and they will fall behind again very soon.

The tragedy is that high-stakes proficiency tests of the kind being increasingly used around the country tend to focus mainly on factual knowledge or general-process skills (reading comprehension, interpretation of graphs and charts, etc.) and not on deep knowledge of concepts or learning abilities and techniques. Since the tests carry high stakes for teachers and school districts as well as for students, and since drilling students using low-level skills achieves better short-term (and short-lived) results, the temptation is great for schools and teachers to use just those methods. As a result, they forego the more sophisticated teaching methods that require students to use inquiry-based learning methods, although such methods have a much greater long-term beneficial impact on students.

But one of the most subtle and pernicious effects of these kinds of low-level teaching methods is that they bore students and turn them away from learning even more. Since the pressure of high-stakes testing is greater on lower-performing schools, students in such schools are more likely to be receiving such teaching, resulting in yet lower achievement in the long run. The vicious cycle is complete.

I live in the small, fairly well-to-do, and ethnically integrated Cleveland suburb of Shaker Heights. It is a community that is deeply committed to achieving equity in education while maintaining high standards. But a community meeting held a few years ago illustrates how myths about the achievement gap dominate discussions of the problem and cause deep divisions even among people sincerely committed to getting together to solve the problem.

A large crowd of residents had come to listen to John Ogbu (professor of anthropology at the University of California, Berkeley) speak on "Schools, Culture, and the Achievement of Minority Children." The meeting in the school auditorium started off peacefully enough, with no hint of the outbursts to come.

Ogbu analyzed the sociological factors that adversely affect the academic performance of African-American and Hispanic students in the American educational system, a subject that has been the cause of much agonized debate among those in the community who had come to realize that minority academic underachievement is a far more intractable problem than perhaps had first been thought.

Although Ogbu's presentation had all the trappings of a college lecture, using flow charts and the models and technical terminology of sociology and anthropology, the ethnically mixed audience of parents, students, teachers, and concerned citizens listened with rapt attention as he addressed a problem that was close to their hearts, for which the absence of a solution was threatening to seriously damage the carefully nurtured racial harmony of the community. Ogbu's important and influential ideas is discussed at some length in chapter 6, but for the moment what is of interest is what happened when he opened the floor for questions and comments at the end of his talk.

As is typical of public meetings on issues of great concern, where the audience has thought a good deal about the issues, the people who spoke up largely ignored the invited speaker and the substance of his presentation. Instead they gave long-winded, rambling, and confused speeches, passionately articulating their own theories based on their experiences with the educational system or on those of their friends and family members.

The theories proposed by the audience members are familiar to anyone who has even cursorily followed the debate on the achievement gap. Standardized tests were attacked as being culturally biased against minority students. Some people blamed low teacher expectations for black students or the lack of sufficient numbers of black teachers to serve as role models and with whom black students could identify. Others pointed to the negative peer pressure that black students encounter (abetted by negative messages from TV and other sources of popular culture) that discourage students from aspiring to academic success. Others blamed large class sizes that created an impersonal atmosphere.

One factor that was identified was the practice of "leveling" (i.e., allowing students and school counselors to decide which level of curriculum difficulty students were comfortable with). Another was "tracking" (i.e., the practice of school districts' using standardized tests on students at an early age and then separating them into different academic streams based on the results of the tests).

Yet others suggested that the learning styles of African-Americans were somehow different from those of whites but that standard teaching methods focused only on those styles that white students possessed and neglected those that advantaged blacks. Some presented a variation of this argument and said there was no achievement gap at all, that people simply had different kinds of intelligences (this idea being loosely derived from the work on multiple intelligences by Howard Gardner[4]) and that the kinds of intelligence African-Americans were strong in was not measured by standard assessment practices.

It was argued that all these factors were leading to a downward spiral of black achievement: poor performance on assessments leading to a large number of black students being channeled into low-ability academic streams, which resulted in even lower levels of achievement.

The speakers did not simply present their theories but also suggested solutions, and the proposed solutions were simple and directly correlated with the suggested causes of the problem: eliminate leveling, tracking, and standardized tests; remove (or at least enlighten) teachers who harbor stereotypes about black-student abilities; increase awareness of black learning styles and intelligences among teachers, and increase the use of teaching methods and assessments that correlate with them; increase the number of black teachers; reduce class sizes; and educate black parents about the importance of monitoring TV, friends, and other potentially negative social influences on their children's lives.

Then came the uproar. It began with a young black graduate of the school system standing up and arguing in an impassioned voice that the problem was quite simple. He said that black students who bought into the value structure of the white community by copying their speech, dress, and economic ambitions did very well in the school system, but that those who wanted to hold on to a semblance of their ethnic identity (by means of dress, speech, and conduct) were ignored. Feeling that the school system did not care about them, these latter black students (whom he said constituted the majority of black students) simply gave up on education, seeking recognition and acceptance in other, nonacademic ways.

When he had finished, a white woman asked what could be done to address these problems, at which point the young man jumped back up and, looking directly at her, said she should learn to *care* for the students who were being rejected by the system. The woman, looking flustered at the surprising personal turn the discussion had taken, nevertheless shot back (to scattered audience applause) that it was precisely because she cared that she even bothered to come to meetings like this to begin with.

Then a white man who identified himself as the father of a biracial child jumped into the fray and angrily charged that it was precisely because white people like this woman (pointing to the same hapless woman who had by now inexplicably become transformed into a symbol of white oppression) did not want to relinquish any of the power that white people controlled, and which had historically oppressed black people, that this situation had arisen. He stormed out of the meeting, again to scattered applause and many audible gasps of astonishment and dismay.

While these heated exchanges were going on, John Ogbu, ostensibly the focus of the evening, looked on with a bemused expression on his face. He looked like someone who had seen this kind of thing many times before.

The meeting dissolved in confusion soon after, with small groups of people clustered together, discussing animatedly, but with worried expressions on their faces. Thus ended another typically volatile, contentious, and ultimately inconclusive discussion about the causes of black educational underachievement, full of charges and countercharges, leaving a residue of anger, resentment, guilt, and a whole lot of uncertainty and anxiety as to how to deal with a perplexing and troublesome issue. Well-meaning people who had come together to address a real problem ended up feeling divided and confused.

The causes and solutions for the academic achievement gap articulated at this meeting have been repeated in all forums, ranging from community meetings to newspaper editorials to scholarly seminars, with similarly inconclusive results. The fact that there exists an achievement gap is indisputable and hardly shocking news. It is a well-studied and established fact that, using almost any measure, black and Hispanic students nationwide perform at lower levels compared to whites.

The measures of the achievement gap are broad. The educational achievement gap has narrowed since 1970, but the typical black student still scores below 75 to 85 percent of white students. The gap between blacks and whites appears before children enter kindergarten and persists into adulthood. The gap between black and white students increases as they go though school K–12, even if they start with the same skills (although most do not). Much of this divergence occurs before high school. This effect cannot be explained by differences between schools or differences in their socioeconomic status.[5]

High school graduation rates nationwide are 78 percent for white students, 56 percent for black students, and 54 percent for Latino students. (Note that there is no unique way of defining graduation rates. The figures quoted were obtained by dividing the number of high school graduation diplomas awarded in 1998 by the number of eighth graders in 1993, after adjusting for changes in the student population due to migration.[6]) In 2003, the average black score on the SAT was 857, while the average white score was 1063.[7] But despite all this study and the well-meaning efforts to address it, there has been no solution to the problem, leading some observers to believe that the fundamental causes lie in deep-rooted and broader socioeconomic and political forces that overwhelm any positive effects that purely educational interventions can produce.

The broader factors can be lumped under three categories, but there is no clear consensus on which of these is most responsible for the gap, and favored explanations seem to depend on where one stands on the conventional ideological spectrum. The "liberal" interpretation is that this gap is the result of economic disparities between the two ethnic communities that can be traced back to the legacy of slavery and other forms of oppression that blacks have suffered. Support for this view (which I will call the socioeconomic model) comes from the fact that educational achievement correlates more strongly (although not perfectly) with socioeconomic status than with any other single variable. Adherents of this model argue that, given that the black community lags badly behind the white in both income and net worth, educational disparities must be caused by socioeconomic disparities. The solution suggested by this explanation is to improve the economic situation of blacks by ensuring equality in the employment and business sectors (by means of affirmative action and various forms of set-asides) and investment in black neighborhoods and businesses. In this model's worldview, once economic disparities disappear, educational (and other) disparities will vanish along with them.

Those at the "conservative" end of the ideological spectrum are not convinced that economic disparities are the primary cause of black educational underachievement. As evidence, they point to the fact that some minority groups, such as certain Asian nationalities who are economically worse off than blacks, excel in school. These observers believe that, while the legacy of slavery and segregation was indeed harsh, the civil rights legislation that began in the 1950s has removed all legal road-blocks to black advancement and that we have now achieved a color-blind society. They further argue that programs such as affirmative action are now actually unfair to white people.

The fact that greater economic and educational advancement has not been made by the black community in the post–civil rights era leads these conservative observers to conclude that various social pathologies within the black community must be at fault. These pathologies take the form of unstable families, poor parenting skills, lack of drive and ambition, nega-tive peer pressure, poor choice of role models, high levels of teenage pregnancies, single motherhood, drugs, crime, and lack of parental in-volvement in children's education. It is suggested that all these factors lead to a lack of interest in education among black students.

Believers in this type of explanation (which I call the sociopathologi-cal model) tend to repeatedly lecture black communities about the need for a wholesale spiritual awakening to traditional virtues and the work ethic. While they appreciate the hardships that blacks suffered in the past, their solution is to say (in effect if not in actual wording), "Get over it. The real victims and perpetrators of the old unjust system are dead. Stop dwelling on the past and claiming to be a victim. Pull yourself up by your bootstraps and take advantage of what is now equally available to everyone." This group concedes that, while racial prejudice still ex-ists, it is now essentially a *personal* matter that should be dealt with on a personal leve!. They are fond of repeatedly quoting Martin Luther King's well-known hopeful dream that one day his children would "not be judged by the color of their skin but by the content of their charac-ter." They believe that time has arrived.

But Martin Luther King's analyses of the conditions of black people were broad-ranging and subtle and cannot be fully appreciated based purely on that one quote. He himself was not sanguine that a truly color-blind society would be achieved so easily. King noted that a merely *legal* color-blind society was fairly cheap to obtain. He said, "There are no ex-penses, and no taxes are required, for Negroes to share lunch counters, libraries, parks, hotels, and other facilities with whites."[8] But he pre-sciently warned that when the issue switched to the second phase, from that of simple decency to one of real equality, much of the multiracial support would evaporate as the cost of the remedies for generations of injustice became clear. "The discount education given to Negroes will in the future have to be purchased at full price if quality education is to be realized. Jobs are harder and costlier to create than voting rolls. The eradication of slums housing millions of people is complex far beyond integrating lunch counters."[9]

King realized that generations of slavery and other forms of discrimination and subjugation had taken their toll on the financial, intellectual, and other resources of the African-American who thus required an enormous and concerted effort *from within his own community* to "overcome his deficiencies and his maladjustments."[10] King acknowledged that part of the responsibility for improvement lay with the black community and thus seemed to lend some support to the sociopathological view. But he rejected out of hand the more extreme form of this view (currently enjoying a resurgence) that the poor conditions under which blacks lived "can be explained by the myth of the Negro's innate incapacities, or by the more sophisticated rationalization of his acquired infirmities (family disorganization, poor education, etc.)."[11]

King was no sentimental believer that this appalling state of affairs would disappear by itself once the institutionalized roadblocks had been removed and a legally "color-blind" society had been created. "Depressed living standards for Negroes are not simply the consequence of neglect. . . . They are a structural part of the economic system in the United States. Certain industries and enterprises are based upon a supply of low-paid, under-skilled and immobile nonwhite labor. Hand assembly factories, hospitals, service industries, housework, agricultural operations using itinerant labor would suffer economic trauma, if not disaster, with a rise in wage scales."[12]

In other words, he argued that powerful economic and political interests benefited from the depressed state of poor people and would strenuously resist any attempts to improve things. He realized that achieving equality for African-Americans required a massive expenditure in education, housing, and employment for blacks, but he always emphasized that this must be done within the context of a general antipoverty program meant *for all poor people, of all races and religions.*[13]

Note that although black people suffer from far worse conditions of poverty than whites (there is a huge "poverty gap," so to speak), King was calling for a widespread antipoverty campaign that encompassed all groups. I think this is because he realized that any program that requires resources and is targeted only at powerless minorities (however deserving) is essentially politically unsustainable. Furthermore, I think he realized that the more extreme black poverty was a symptom of a general inequity in social conditions that affects everyone and that this more widespread problem has to be addressed if black poverty is to be reduced. This theme will recur in this book in relation to education. The elimination of the educational gap will occur only in the context of a program to improve the education of students of all ethnicities and that encompasses all socioeconomic categories.

The experience of Shaker Heights (where the above community meeting was held) is interesting because this city seems, at least on the surface, to have avoided both the socioeconomic and the sociopathological causes of black underachievement. The district has received nationwide media attention precisely because it seems to not have the kinds of problems that are commonly identified as leading to achievement gaps. Thus any major educational disparity there (or in similar communities) is especially troubling, which is why the educational achievement gap within this city (and similar cities nationwide) creates such strong feelings.

As implied above, Shaker Heights is not your typical community. It is a small inner-ring bedroom suburb of Cleveland, Ohio, covering an area of about five square miles and having a population of 30,000. It is a carefully planned city, with tree-lined streets winding past well-maintained homes with manicured lawns, lakes, parks, and redbrick schools nestled in campus-like grounds. In the post–civil rights era, it sought to become a model integrated community, encouraging diversity and discouraging white emigration by taking steps to maintain high property values and efficient city services. As a result, the city is now about one-third African-American, with the rest being white (with a sprinkling of other minorities).

The city is proud of its ethnic diversity and goes to great lengths to ensure that civic and community bodies reflect it. Although there is a range of income levels in the city, from the poor (about 10 percent living below the poverty level) to the extremely affluent, and though there are socioeconomic disparities based on ethnicity, its primary image is that of a middle- and upper-middle-class integrated community (with a median family income of about $80,000), home to many of the academics, professionals, and corporate executives of all ethnic groups who work in the Cleveland area. It is also a highly educated community, with 60 percent of all residents over the age of 25 holding at least a bachelor's degree. This is *three times* the national average.

It is also a community that prides itself on the excellence of its school systems (city motto: "A community is known by the schools it keeps"), voting in favor of extra school levies every few years so that it has one of the highest tax rates in the state of Ohio. This enables the school district to provide a wide range of academic and extracurricular programs that provide the students who take advantage of them with an education that would be the envy of any child in the nation. Hence the city tends to attract as residents relatively well-off, educationally ambitious people who seek both an integrated community and a high-quality education for their children. To attend a school orchestra or band function, with an overflowing audience consisting of all ethnic groups watching and playing together in harmony, is to see a model of what America as a whole might be if it could put its racial tensions behind it.

And every year, the school district sends off about 85 percent of its graduating seniors to four-year colleges, many of them prestigious, among them a remarkably high number of National Merit Scholarship semifinalists, considerably out of proportion to the size of its student enrollment. The 2004 high school graduating class had 25 semifinalists out of a class of 350, whereas, taking the national average, such a class would normally be expected to have just one or two semifinalists. The *Wall Street Journal*, in a nationwide 2003 survey of high schools that sent the largest percentage of its graduating seniors to Ivy League colleges, found that the Shaker Heights High School was the only school in Ohio (private, parochial, or public) that made the list of top-65 schools.[14]

On the surface, then, this is a community that seems to have solved the problem of ethnic divisiveness that plagues the rest of the country. It has no deep economic or social problems. It is ethnically integrated, with the school-student population almost evenly split in numbers between black and white students. And by any conventional measure it has an excellent school system that provides equal access to students of all ethnicities. But there is trouble beneath the surface, and the educational achievement gap is the indicator.

As would be expected given its advantageous demographics, black Shaker students on average do better than black students elsewhere in the state and nation, just as white students do better than their counterparts in most other school systems. The real puzzle has been why, although both communities have equal access to all the school district's educational opportunities, the academic performance of black Shaker students lags significantly behind those of white Shaker students. For example, the average black SAT score in 2003 was 926 (compared to a nationwide black average of 857), while that of white students was 1220 (compared to a nationwide white average of 1063).[15]

There are other symptoms of the problem that immediately become visible when you walk into some high school classrooms. In the highest-achievement tracks (the advanced-placement sections) you find only a handful of black students (about 10 percent or even less), while the lowest-achievement tracks (called general education) have them almost exclusively (about 95 percent).

In February 1997, the high school newspaper, *The Shakerite*, also blazoned the results of a survey across its front page. The survey showed among other things that 84 percent of all D and F grades awarded were earned by black students, and that 92 percent of students who failed one or more subjects of the state proficiency tests and who earned at least one D or F grade were black. The grade point average of black students was 2.20, while that of white students was 3.34, and so on. The differences were startling and triggered calls for an investigation of the causes. This was what prompted the invitation to John Ogbu to study the causes of the achievement gap in Shaker Heights and resulted in the stormy community meeting.

For concerned members of the community, the question that lies at the forefront of their minds is one posed starkly by a worried black woman during the same Ogbu community meeting: "In this community we have large numbers of black families which provide stable two-parent households and in which both parents are well-to-do, educated professionals, upholding all the virtues that are assumed to be the important for their children's educational success. And yet the children of these black families still seem to underperform when compared with similar white families. What is going on?"

The unspoken concern is that if the educational achievement gap cannot be closed in a community that is middle-class, integrated, provides equal access to all students, and has a commitment to quality education, what hope is there for the rest of the country? Is there something inherently insoluble about this problem? What, indeed, is going on?

And therein lies the crux of the problem. It is easy to think one understands the causes of the educational achievement gap when one has a mental image of black students as coming from urban and poor dysfunctional families, and of white students as being suburban and middle- or upper-class. But not all students fit this stereotype, and the achievement gap transcends all these categories. For example, black students from families with incomes of more than $100,000 had a mean SAT score that was 142 points below the mean score for whites from families at the same income level.[16] As we will see in later chapters, neither the socioeconomic nor the sociopathological model seems to be able to account for all the differences in achievement.

This failure has been used to garner support for the third view (which I will call the genetic model), which in its most extreme form is represented by Charles Murray and Richard Herrnstein, authors of *The Bell Curve*, which focused on the 15-point difference in average IQ scores between blacks and whites.[17] After making the appropriate regretful noises to indicate their lack of racial prejudice, the authors essentially conclude that the educational disparity is a fact of nature, the result of long-term evolutionary selectivity that has resulted in blacks' simply not having the genetic raw material to compete equally with whites. These authors argue that instead of well-meaning, heroic, but ultimately futile efforts to solve an inherently insoluble problem, the best thing to do is to accept this situation as a fact of life and then determine how to minimize its adverse social consequences.

So the reasons for the educational achievement gap are seen as arising from three possible causes: socioeconomic, sociopathological, and genetic, or some combination of the three. This book will examine the research into these and other possible causes of the educational achievement gap and the effectiveness of the solutions that have been attempted. In the process of doing so, we will investigate many of the myths about the causes of the gap. The difficulty with myths is that they are not necessarily false but are beliefs whose truth or reality is accepted uncritically. It is relatively easy to debunk outright falsehoods. Much harder to overcome are those beliefs that have some element of truth in them (like the ones raised at the community meeting) but the obsession with which can undermine attempts to systematically solve the problem.

In the next three chapters I will argue that the genetic, socioeconomic, and sociopathological models (and their associated myths) do not completely explain the gap and that we need to look beyond these familiar modes of thinking if we are to make any real headway in solving the problem.

NOTES

1. CNN.com/Education, "Supporters Hail Affirmative Action Ruling," June 24, 2003, www.cnn.com/2003/EDUCATION/06/24/affirmative.action.michigan.ap.

2. James Baldwin, *The Fire Next Time* (New York: Dial Press, 1963), 108.

3. *The Black Commentator*, "The Jayson Blair/New York Times Affair," May 15, 2003, www.blackcommentator.com/42/42_cover.html.

4. Howard Gardner, *Multiple Intelligences: The Theory in Practice* (New York: Basic Books, 1993).

5. Christopher Jencks and Meredith Phillips, "The Black–White Test Score Gap: An Introduction," in *The Black–White Test Score Gap*, ed. Christopher Jencks and Meredith Phillips (Washington, DC: Brookings Institution Press, 1998), 1.

6. Jay P. Greene, "High School Graduation Rates in the United States," The Manhattan Institute for Policy Research, www.manhattan-institute.org/html/cr_baeo.htm#04.

7. For more data on disparities, see the Web site of *The Journal of Blacks in Higher Education*, July 17, 2003, www.jbhe.com/vital/index.html.

8. Martin Luther King Jr., *Where Do We Go from Here: Chaos or Community* (Boston: Beacon Press, 1968), 5.

9. King Jr., *Where Do We Go from Here*, 6.

10. King Jr., *Where Do We Go from Here*, 9.

11. King Jr., *Where Do We Go from Here*, 7.

12. King Jr., *Where Do We Go from Here*, 7.

13. Interview with *Playboy* magazine in 1965, published in James M. Washington, ed., *Testament of Hope* (San Francisco: Harper and Row, 1986), 386.

14. Elizabeth Bernstein, "The Price of Admission," *Wall Street Journal*, 2 April 2004, W1.

15. Dale Whittington, *Shaker Heights Fact Book 2002–2003*, private communication.

16. See the Web site of *The Journal of Blacks in Higher Education*, July 17, 2003, www.jbhe.com/vital/index.html.

17. Richard J. Herrnstein and Charles Murray, *The Bell Curve: Intelligence and Class Structure in American Life* (New York: Free Press, 1994).

4

THE CASE AGAINST THE GENETIC MODEL

When I was growing up in Sri Lanka, my grandfather had a very simple explanation for why at that time our own ethnic group (the Tamils) was overrepresented in the universities and in the prestigious professions. He asserted that Tamils were simply smarter than others. It seemed self-evident to him that if one group of people consistently did disproportionately well academically, and assuming there was no systematic bias or fraud in their favor, then that group must be smarter than the rest. What other explanation could there be?

There is nothing that bedevils any discussion about education and the achievement gap than this kind of belief. The idea that the people of the world can be classified in terms of some *intrinsic* and inherited quality of "smartness" and that this determines their academic success is deeply entrenched in popular culture. It is believed that smarter people learn more, learn faster, and learn more deeply. From this it is only a short step to argue that if one recognizably different group of people performs consistently better than another, then the first group must possess the smartness quality in greater measure. In the United States, this line of reasoning leads to the conclusion that whites are smarter than blacks.

But this last short step in reasoning is rarely explicitly taken (at least publicly) anymore because of the explosive political nature of its conclusions. But that does not mean the belief is not held privately. Evidence for its covert existence can be seen in the way that people seized on this type of conclusion when it was once again proposed in the book *The Bell Curve* by Murray and Herrnstein when it was published in 1994. The book received wide prepublication publicity, and initial reporting on the book treated it as if it were a work of science and as if its conclusions were widely supported within the scientific community.

The authors of this book asserted that the present state of social inequality, rather than being due to a form of class tyranny with entrenched wealth perpetuating itself by using its social and economic power, was actually caused by the unequal distribution of intelligence. In other words, we are supposedly living in a meritocracy where rewards are distributed according to the amount of intelligence one possesses. This argument is basically a more sophisticated variant of my grandfather's more simply stated belief.

Murray and Herrnstein argue in support of the existence of a single, general intelligence measure (called Spearman's *g*), which can be estimated using intelligence quotient (or IQ) tests. They seem to find that intelligence correlates with IQ and that IQ is substantially genetic, heritable, and unchangeable. They breezily assert that there is a consensus amongst the psychometric community that the genetic contribution to IQ is in the range of 40 to 80 percent, and they use the mean value of 60 percent for their analyses.

They also seem to find that people with low IQ cause most of the problems of society, such as welfare dependency, crime, divorce, illegitimacy, poor parenting, and unemployment, while those at the top of society's ladder have high IQs. In other words, IQ, education, income, and wealth are all positively correlated, and the current state of society is the result of this meritocracy in action. To try and tamper with its results was to encourage mediocrity and disturb the natural order of things.

The authors pondered the consequences of their results, and they did not shy away from the policy implications that naturally follow. If success in life is so determined by IQ, and if IQ is largely immutable, then it is foolish to waste precious resources in a well-meaning but misguided effort to lift the poor out of their state by giving them assistance based on the assumption that they are as able as everyone else. It would be far better to accept that the inferior lot of these people is determined by natural factors and that we should simply make sure they are kept out of trouble and misery.

There is more. The authors say we should focus our efforts on making sure that the "cognitively gifted" (i.e., those with high IQ scores) get all the resources necessary to enable them to reach their full potential, since it is from this group that society can expect to reap any real benefit. They even argue that, when intelligence is taken into account, the people who are currently successful are actually the ones who are discriminated against, because their rewards are not commensurate with their intelligence. So they recommend that educational resources *be taken away from the disadvantaged and given to the gifted* by means of school choice, vouchers, tax credits, and scholarships. They also recommend abolishing affirmative action as we know it in higher education and the workplace and discouraging births by low-IQ women. The book essentially advocates consigning an entire class of people, nominally based on IQ but effectively based largely on ethnicity, to the status of a permanent underclass with no hope for advancement.

The authors also recommend, without any sense of irony or *déjà vu*, limiting immigration so that low-IQ immigrants are kept out of the United States. This was not the first time that IQ scores were recommended as an instrument of social policy. There had been earlier attempts to use them for military recruitment and selection of the officer corps, and there had also been attempts to set immigration policy based on the intelligence of various ethnic groups. In the 1920s, these same arguments were used to shut out Jews and Slavic groups as potential immigrants because of their low IQ scores.[1] But the fact that these groups are no longer considered inferior does not seem to give Murray and Herrnstein pause for concern that these arguments applied in the contemporary context may also suffer from the same flaws.

It can be speculated that the reason the book gained a large and (at least initially) uncritical readership was because the authors took advantage of the fact that their thesis was appealing to a lot of people, especially those at the top of the achievement pyramid. Such arguments can usually count on some measure of support from elite circles because they pander to their self-image. These arguments say that the people and groupings that dominate our society do so because of their intrinsic ability, that this is the way things are meant to be, and that these people should benefit even more. It is nice to be told that the reason one is successful is because one is smarter than others, not because of inherited advantages of wealth, social and family connections, color, and other forms of privilege. It gives people the comforting notion that we live in a world where innate ability is rewarded. The book stamped these beliefs with the "science" seal of approval, thus making its conclusions socially acceptable, despite the deeply negative consequences they entailed for the various minority ethnic groupings adversely affected by them.

But this recent incarnation of an old idea was particularly brazen in its formulation, and this may have been the reason for the ferocity of the opposition to it that eventually arose. Subsequent analysis of the book has shown it to be shoddy scholarship in the pursuit of a dubious political agenda. As Nicholas Lehman asserts, *The Bell Curve*, it turns out, is full of mistakes ranging from sloppy reasoning to mis-citations of sources to outright mathematical errors. Unsurprisingly, all the mistakes are in the direction of supporting the authors' thesis." One example is that the actual consensus range of the genetic contribution to IQ is actually 30 to 50 percent, lower than the 40 to 80 percent asserted by Murray and Herrnstein.[2] Scholars pounced on the book's many weaknesses, and its main theses have been discredited.[3]

But the mere fact that such a book gained such widespread acceptance (at least initially) is a sign that there exists fertile soil for these ideas and that many people already harbor vague suspicions to that effect. If we really seek the elimination of the achievement gap, it is necessary to firmly refute these ideas and understand clearly the reasons for the refutation, since they undermine any educational efforts to solve the problem. "Once hereditarianism percolates into popular culture, it can easily become an excuse for treating academic failure as an inescapable fact of nature."[4]

In a broader sense, this whole discussion is pointless because, "[f]or the past several decades, biological anthropologists have been arguing that races don't really exist, or, more precisely, that the concept of race has no validity as a biological category."[5] Biologists have found that trying to link traditional concepts of racial groupings according to their biology is a hopeless task because the genetic variation among even relatively small groups of people is so great that it becomes impossible to find identifiable biological markers that correlate with these traditional groupings. For example, even if everyone on Earth became extinct except for the Kikuyu of East Africa, it would still be possible to reconstitute 85 percent of human genetic variation.[6]

Of course one can always find some superficial characteristics that are shared by people who live in geographically localized areas, due to adaptation to the local environment and other causes. For example, similar hair texture, hair and skin color, and nose and eye features are shared by people who live in Africa or the Far East. But using these features to classify races is impossible to justify because all these features are also shared by people in other parts of the world, and other genetic variations overwhelm these minor, but visibly obvious, differences. It would be almost as arbitrary as classifying races according to similarities in eye color or height or blood type.[7]

The only sensible way to think of race is to see it as a socially constructed entity based on language, culture, and other features that over time are shared by groups of people. The word ethnicity captures this sense of commonality better, even though the word *race* (with all its spurious biological implications) is probably here to stay as a means of distinguishing between ethnic groups.

The fact that "race" does not exist as a meaningful category does not mean that the problems of race have magically disappeared or that we can ignore differences in performance between different groupings based on these outmoded categorizations. Looking at how different ethnic groupings such as black and white students fare in education gives us important information about the state of social justice in our societies and about how resources are distributed. It is just that looking for *biological causes* for these differences is unlikely to yield anything useful.

Let us start with those things that we can (perhaps) agree on. There is some quality called intelligence that people possess. We all have some intuitive idea of how this quality manifests itself in people. Clearly, we associate this quality with learning. Think for a moment of those people whom you think of as "intelligent." The chances are you will recall your high-achieving classmates in school or college or those people with high levels of education. People who learn new things quickly and more deeply are perceived as being more intelligent than others. There are

other popular indicators of intelligence, such as verbal and written flu-
ency, an easy facility with mathematics, or skills in reasoning and argu-
mentation.

But while we all have some intuitive idea of what intelligence is,
quantifying it and measuring it have been much more problematic. Ever
since the concept of IQ was invented by Alfred Binet in 1908 and a test
was devised to measure it, this particular measure has been popularly
perceived as a major indicator of an individual's intellectual capabilities,
a measure of what a person is capable of cognitively. The concept has
achieved a mystique in the United States that would be unrecognizable
to Binet, who had a much more modest conception of it as a diagnostic
tool to see if children were keeping up with their schoolwork.[8] But the
status of IQ has grown so much over time that in some circles it is even
used as a badge of honor, and an organization exists (Mensa) to which
only members who score in the top 2 percent on IQ tests are eligible to
belong.

But among professional psychometricians, the meaning of the IQ
score has been more problematic, and debates have raged over whether
the characteristic that we popularly refer to as "intelligence" can be effectively measured by simple cognitive tests and assigned a single score
that can be used to rank people. Even conceding such a quality, other
debates continue over such things as whether intelligence is immutable
or whether it can change and the extent to which genes and environment compete in the formation of intelligence.

No one seriously argues in favor of either of the two extreme views,
that a person's intelligence is influenced exclusively by either genes or
by the environment. Both are deemed to play a role, and the relative
weight that each contributes is a scientifically interesting question to investigate. This so-called nature–nurture controversy has centered
around how much each factor contributes, with estimates of the role of
"nature" (i.e., genes) varying widely. Pinning down this number more
precisely has proven to be understandably difficult. After all, not only is
intelligence hard to define and measure, but human beings are not easily studied under artificially controlled conditions that can separate out
the influence of the environment. All of this makes it extremely hard to
disentangle the effects of genes and environment in a human being's development.

In order to compensate for the lack of laboratory-style experimentation, studies in this area have had to rely on a variety of naturally occurring situations to infer the relative contributions of genes and environments to IQ. They have studied such things as identical twins separated at birth (very rare occurrences); parent–child and sibling–sibling IQ correlations in families that have a combination of full siblings, half siblings, and adopted children; mixed-race adoptions; children of black and white U.S. soldiers in Germany; and so forth. The results that emerge from all these studies are mixed, to say the least, which allows for the existing wide range of conclusions.

Even if one could arrive at a consensus on the relative contributions of genes and environment to a person's intelligence, and even if one conceded that the genetic contribution was in the high range claimed by Murray and Herrnstein (say 60 percent or above), this still would not justify saying that little can be done to improve the conditions of low-IQ people. This is because the mere fact that a quality is genetic does not mean that it is immutable or that its effects cannot be overcome. For example, the natural color of one's hair is a 100 percent inherited quality. But hair color can be changed quite easily, so if there were a decided advantage to having blonde hair, the disadvantage that comes with being born brunette could be easily compensated for by artificial means.

While hair color can be dismissed as a trivial example because there is no evidence that it is linked with intelligence, a feature that perhaps functions in a manner closer to intelligence is eyesight. While environment (in the form of nutrition or good lighting conditions) can play a role in the quality of sight an adult has, having good eyesight is also undoubtedly a largely genetic quality, and modern society sets a high premium on it. There is almost no aspect of life that does not involve sight. This could have devastating effects on the performance of a person with naturally poor eyesight. But simple devices like eyeglasses or contact lenses almost completely compensate for this deficiency and enable the wearer to compete on an even footing with those for whom genes confer excellent eyesight. There is no real premium attached by society to whether a person's twenty-twenty vision is due mostly to genes or to the use of corrective lenses. Society treats both kinds of people as functionally equivalent, and rightly so. So even if intelligence is substantially genetic, this has no substantial consequences unless one can also show that there are no mechanisms that can compensate for natural disadvantages. But education can play such a compensating role.

Another problem that needs to be addressed is the relationship between individual genetic variation and group variation, since this is the source of one of the most common fallacies that occur in this debate. The fallacious reasoning goes something like this: if the variation in any particular individual trait is caused by genes, then the difference in average values of the trait in populations must be caused by genes too. From this we conclude that the differences in average values of the trait for the groups provide a measure of the differences in average values of the trait in individuals. This is my grandfather's argument again.

At first blush, this line of reasoning seems impeccable, which is one reason why the genetic argument is so strongly present in discussions of the achievement gap. After all, there is no doubt that average IQ scores of blacks are 15 points lower than those of whites. So if IQ scores serve as proxy measures for intelligence, surely this difference in average scores must be because whites have, on average, higher intelligence than blacks.

However plausible this sounds initially, the fallacy of this logic becomes immediately obvious with a little thought and the use of a popular analogy. If we randomly take some corn seed and plant it in rich, well-tended soil, we will get a distribution of plant heights whose variation is entirely due to the variations in individual genes. If we take a sample of seed from the *same* source (i.e., from the identical gene pool) and plant it in poor soil, we will again get a variation of heights that is almost entirely due to genes. But the second group will have a lower average height than the first, even though they come from the same gene pool. This difference in average values of height for the two samples is caused entirely by the environment (the soil) and not the genes, a fact known to every farmer. The corn is the same in both cases.

So it is possible to have variation in some trait within a *single* group that is due purely to genes, while the differences in average values of the same trait between different groups is caused purely by environment. For example, the variation in individual heights of people has a substantial genetic component. But in Japan, which has been a relatively isolated country, average heights have risen considerably since World War II, a fact easily explainable by better nutrition. So looking at differences in averages between groups cannot be used to infer genetic dis-tributions of individual traits *unless we can be sure that the environment has been the same for both groups.*

The IQ debate is an old one, usually waged in academic circles, but occasionally spreading into the public arena when IQ scores have been used to set public policy. It is safe to say that despite decades of effort by very determined people, we are not much closer to a definitive an-swer to the question of the role of race and intelligence in the social and economic stratification of society. All kinds of different hypotheses, based on varying genetic and environmental combinations, can be in-voked to explain the data. This is, perhaps, not surprising. After all, both race and intelligence are poorly defined and operationally ambiguous concepts. When you have two variables that are ill-defined, it is asking too much to expect a simple relationship between them to emerge.

But more damaging to the idea of genes as the determinant of intel-ligence and IQ have been studies showing that education has a big ef-fect on IQ scores. IQ scores show an increase of up to 2.5 points for *each year of education*.[9] As a child goes through K–12 school, on average their IQ can increase by over 30 points. So the argument that the 15-point IQ difference between blacks and whites is due to differences in education and other environmental factors is quite plausible. In fact, just a six-year difference in schooling can produce the 15-point gap. While the difference in the actual number of years of school attended by black and white students may not be as large as six, when one con-siders the number of years of *effective* schooling that each group re-ceives (based on the quality of instruction and resources available to the two groups), the 15-point gap becomes a lot less mysterious.

Other studies testify to the importance of schooling in influencing IQ scores. Studies of riverboat captains' children who attended school in-termittently found that the scores rose when they attended school and dropped during their prolonged absences.[10]

But it is perhaps the work of researcher James R. Flynn that provides the most persuasive argument that the 15-point gap in IQ scores is not the huge, insurmountable genetic barrier that *The Bell Curve* implies.[11] To understand the significance of his work, it has to be appreciated that av-erage IQ scores for the population are normed each time so that the av-erage values always come out to be 100. Having an unchanging average score is convenient because it enables one to immediately conclude from someone's score how that person compares with the average. This enables us to consistently describe scores below 100 as "below normal" and scores above 100 as "above normal." But what is often overlooked is that these judgments are valid only for comparisons between people who take the *same* IQ test. But IQ tests change over time. The question then arises, if someone scores 110 on a test designed and normed in, say, 1950, does that person necessarily have an IQ above normal in the year 2000?

Flynn analyzed the variation in IQ test results for several nations over a long period of time and found that IQ tests had become progressively *more difficult*. By giving the historically different tests (each normed in its own time to have an average of 100) to the same group of people and comparing scores obtained by these people on tests developed at different times in the past, he could estimate how much IQ scores had to be adjusted over time to maintain the average score at 100. He found that average IQ scores have risen by five points every 15 years, or by one-third of a point each year. So a 15-point rise in scores (which is the size of the gap in black–white IQ scores) can be achieved within a 45-year period. If there is one thing we know about human evolution, it is that it is a really, really slow process, so this rapid rise in IQ scores cannot be explained by changes in the genetic pool.

But what we do know is that access to education has been exploding over the past few decades. When coupled with other studies on the role of education in generating increased IQ, it is not unreasonable to assume that the average increase in IQ scores over time is due to the more widespread education that has become available.

So what is one to make of all these studies? All one can say is that while determining the exact proportions that genes and environment contribute to a person's intelligence is a valid and interesting question for scientific study, the present state of the field does not really offer a definitive answer. Furthermore, the proposition that the amount and quality of education one receives plays an important role in determining one's intelligence is one that has to be taken seriously. We seem to come back to the idea that education looms more importantly than ever. In other words, education can be considered as "eyeglasses for the mind," something that can compensate for unequal genetic distributions and enable people of different "natural" intelligence to compete equally. So people with low IQs should not be separated and further marginalized, as recommended by Murray and Herrnstein. They should instead be the beneficiaries of a good educational program.

NOTES

1. Stephen Jay Gould, *The Mismeasure of Man* (New York: W. W. Norton and Co., 1981).

2. Nicholas Lehman, "The Bell Curve Flattened," *Slate*, January 18, 1997, http://slate.msn.com/id/2416/#sb50882.

3. See Steve Fraser, ed., *The Bell Curve Wars: Race, Intelligence, and the Future of America* (New York: Basic Books, 1995).

4. Christopher Jencks and Meredith Phillips, "America's Next Achievement Test," *The American Prospect* 9, no. 40 (September 1998), www.prospect .org/print-friendly/print/V9/40/jencks-c.html.

5. Carol Mukhopadhyay and Rosemary C. Henze, "How Real Is Race?" *Phi Delta Kappan* (May 2003): 669–78.

6. R. C. Lewontin, Steven Rose, and Leon J. Kamin, *Not in Our Genes* (New York: Pantheon Books, 1984), 126.

7. Mukhopadhyay and Henze, "How Real Is Race?"

8. Gould, *The Mismeasure of Man*.

9. Lehman, "The Bell Curve Flattened."

10. Gerald W. Bracey, "Getting Smart(er) in School," *Phi Delta Kappan* (January 1992): 414–15; Joseph F. Fagan and Cynthia Holland, "Equal Opportunity and Racial Differences in IQ," *Intelligence* 30 (2002): 361–87.

11. James R. Flynn, "Massive IQ Gains in 14 Nations," *Psychological Bulletin* 101, no. 2 (1987): 171–91; and James R. Flynn, "The Mean IQ of Americans: Massive Gains 1932 to 1978," *Psychological Bulletin* 95, no. 1 (1984): 29–51.

5

INCOME, WEALTH, AND THE ACHIEVEMENT GAP

There is no doubt that historical discrimination patterns based on ethnicity have been the cause of huge gaps in wealth between blacks and whites. The long and cruel history of slavery prevented wealth accumulation among black people, so the net assets held by the black community are far fewer than those of whites. Even if employment and education discrimination were to magically disappear so that no income gap existed, blacks would still be disadvantaged because of the wealth gap. This is an important fact that tends to be overlooked by those who argue that the removal of most legal roadblocks to equality in education and employment has now given everyone an equal chance of success and that, hence, the present lower socioeconomic status of blacks must be due to their own faults.

To understand why this line of thinking is incorrect, consider the analogy of a poker game in which two players of equal skill and starting with equal amounts of money play against each other. One player cheats, however, and uses this unfair advantage over time to acquire most of the money, while the other player is pushed to the verge of bankruptcy and elimination. At this point, the two players are replaced by their two children, who are also equally skilled at the game. The child of the cheater truthfully says that he is ashamed of his parent's cheating and is not going to cheat anymore but will play the game fairly henceforth. However, this still does not mean that the two new players now have equal chances of winning.

The player who has a lot of reserve cash has many more options for action at his disposal; he can take more risks and be more adventurous, all the while knowing that occasional failures, or even a string of failures, are not fatal. This player would need a long streak of bad luck to go bankrupt. The player who is initially almost bankrupt, on the other hand, has no such freedom, since even a small streak of bad luck could result in her elimination from the game. So the second player has to be much more cautious and thus has fewer options. The chances of just getting back to an even footing with the other player, let alone winning, are very slim. She needs a long streak of extremely good luck just to reach parity with her opponent.

So simply declaring that henceforth all ethnic groups will be treated equally and fairly (even if this were actually carried out) does not mean that everyone has an equal chance of success. Inherited accumulated wealth carries with it advantages that tilt the odds heavily in favor of those who have it.

There is no question that, on average, the black community is poorer than the white community, both in terms of the assets they possess and in terms of their income. A report entitled *The State of the Dream 2004*,[1] released by the group United for a Fair Economy, which got its data from publicly available census and other government sources, determines that "in 2001, the typical Black household had a net worth of just $19,000 (including home equity) compared with $121,000 for whites. Blacks had 16% of the median wealth of whites, up from 5% in 1989." Also, "[f]or every dollar of white per capita income, African Americans had 55 cents in 1968—and only 57 cents in 2001."

As we have shown in previous chapters, on average, black students achieve at lower levels than white students. Taken in conjunction with wealth and income disparities, there clearly exist positive correlations between income (or wealth) and educational achievement for the different ethnic groups. It is tempting to draw some seemingly obvious conclusions from these incontrovertible pieces of information and to infer that causal connections exist amongst them, and many people have not hesitated to draw such mistaken conclusions.[2]

One of the conclusions frequently inferred is that cause-and-effect relationships between ethnicity, income/wealth differentials, and educational underachievement go in the direction of saying that somehow "blackness" causes underachievement. We then have two choices. One is that this is a biological phenomenon, that black people are genetically predisposed to lower levels of educational achievement and that this in turn leads to lower levels of income and wealth. The arguments in favor of this biological point of view have, I hope, been convincingly refuted in the previous chapter. The second choice is that this is a cultural phenomenon, that there is something going on in the black community that works against high educational achievement. This sociopathological view is addressed in the next chapter.

In this chapter, we will examine the other often-inferred causal relationship, between income/wealth and educational achievement, to see if the differences in the former are the cause of the latter. In other words, can the differences in income and wealth between blacks and whites account for the differences in educational achievement?

The short answer to this question is, only partially. This may be a disappointment for many well-meaning people because of their feeling that the socioeconomic explanation of the achievement gap is more inoffensive than the other two possibilities. The genetic explanation seems racist and unchangeable, while the sociopathological explanation seems accusatory and insulting toward the black community. However, the fact that there is not a strong causal link between socioeconomic status and academic achievement actually provides hope that we will be able to address the problem.

The typical measure used in the social sciences to determine the role of income and wealth is an index called "socioeconomic status" (SES). It turns out that there is no unique or standard way of defining and measuring SES, and measures of socioeconomic status usually take into account parental education in addition to income and wealth. But even using this expanded measure of SES accounts for, at most, one-third of the gap.[3]

Broader measures of SES can be invoked (which include grandparents' educational attainment, mother's household size, mother's high school quality, mother's perceived self-efficacy, children's birth weight, and children's household size), and these explain about half of the gap.[4] But clearly, when we begin to use such broad measures, we rapidly enter into the social and cultural sphere, where the values of the community come into play. This issue will be discussed in the next chapter.

Even if it were true that SES is the major cause of the educational achievement gap, this would not mean that the only way to erase the gap is to erase all SES differences. There are purely educational strategies that provide promise of eliminating the educational achievement gap. If this can be done, then it opens up the possibility of eliminating the income gap and, in the long-term, the SES gap. In other words, it may be possible to reverse the causal relationships and turn the problem into the solution. Thus, even if SES differences are the cause of the educational achievement gap, it may be that eliminating the educational achievement gap by primarily educational measures will enable us to eliminate the SES gap.

The difficulty of trying to achieve full equality the other way around (by first aiming for income and wealth equality) can be seen by looking at the changes (or lack of them) in income and wealth data over the years. As cited earlier in this chapter, in 1968, blacks earned 55 cents for every dollar of white income; in 2001, they earned 57 cents. At the current rate, it would take 581 years to close the income gap. Similarly, at the current rate, we would have to wait until the year 2099 to reach parity in wealth.

If closing black–white income and wealth differences is the only way to close the achievement gap, then we are in serious trouble because those gaps seem to be extremely resistant to change. Fortunately, black–white income differences have only a small effect on test scores.[5]

One statistic that surprises some people is that the typical black child and the typical white child live in school districts that spend almost the same average amount per pupil.[6] This seems to contradict our mental image of black students going to underfunded urban schools while white students attend well-supplied suburban schools. There are two reasons that costs get equalized. One is that children in poor rural districts are mostly white, and these numbers compensate for the high amounts spent on white suburban children. The second reason is that urban schools tend to have larger costs that go toward noneducational services (such as transportation, cost of living, school-provided meals) or toward the more expensive education of special-needs children.

One of the most interesting, but little-known, studies is by Clifford Adelman at the U.S. Department of Education, who did a detailed analysis of the factors that play a role in determining bachelor's degree completion rates.[7] He used data generated by the High School and Beyond/Sophomore Cohort longitudinal study, which followed a national sample of 28,000 students from 1980 (when they were high school sophomores) until 1993 (when they had reached an age of roughly 30) to see what factors affected college graduation rates. He found that, although the college-access gap for blacks and Latinos had closed over the previous two decades, the degree-completion gap remained at 20 percent or higher. What is interesting is that socioeconomic status provides only a modest contribution to this gap, and the race/ethnicity variable matters very, very little.

So what *does* matter? What determines the degree-completion gap? Adelman found that a measure defined as "academic resources" (made up of a composite of high school curriculum, test scores, and class rank) has much greater predictive power than does SES in predicting college-degree completion. For example, students in the lowest two SES quintiles, but with the highest academic resources, graduated at higher rates than the majority of students in the highest SES quintile. He also found that the impact of high school curriculum was far more pronounced *positively* for black and Latino students than was any other measure and that it consistently overwhelmed demographic variables such as gender, race, and SES. In other words, improving the high school curriculum had a *disproportionately* positive effect on underachieving minority students.

Studies such as these provide hope for the future. If SES were the primary cause of educational achievement, then closing the gap would lie outside the province of educators. We would have to wait around, treading water, hoping that some broader, national economic and social forces would come into play and close the SES gap. I don't think this is likely to occur. As discussed earlier, the economic gap has barely closed at all over the past four decades.

Furthermore, there are currently strong bipartisan forces pushing in the direction of maintaining or even *increasing* economic inequality. The tax policies of the last decade have resulted in a further shifting of wealth toward the upper income bracket. In his book *Perfectly Legal* (which should be required reading for anyone interested in the way tax policies are skewing the distribution of wealth and income for the benefit of those who already have a lot of it), author David Cay Johnson says,

> Now, less than a century after its adoption, the tax system is being turned on its head. Since at least 1983 it has been the explicit, but unstated, policy in Washington to let the richest Americans pay a smaller portion of their incomes in taxes and to defer more of their taxes, which amounts to a stealth tax cut, while collecting more in taxes from those in the middle class.
>
> The Democrats embraced this in 1983, when they controlled Congress. They voted to raise Social Security taxes, changing it from a pay-as-you-go system to one in which people were required to pay 50 percent more than the retirement and disability program's immediate costs, to build a trust fund to pay benefits more than three decades into the future. Those taxes were not, however, locked away but instead were spent to help finance tax cuts for the super rich that began in 1981.
>
> Under the Republicans, beginning in 1997, this policy of taxing the poor and the middle class to finance tax cuts for the super rich was expanded through changes in the income tax system. The changes were subtle and hardly reported in the news media, but they were also substantial. Under the first round of Bush tax cuts enacted in 2001 the middle class and the upper middle class will subsidize huge tax cuts for the top 1 percent, and, especially the top one-tenth of 1 percent, the 130,000 richest taxpayers.
>
> For a nation that has debated for years whether the tax rate cuts begun by President Reagan in 1981 are "trickle-down economics," it may be startling to read that the reality of these changes has been just the reverse. The tax system is causing the benefits of American society to flow up and pool at the top.[8]

But if there are *educational* measures that can be taken to close the achievement gap, then such measures are within our control, and we can use them to counter antiegalitarian forces. Achieving this is not going to be easy. It will require not only changes in teaching practices (which are hard enough), but also changes in the way we think about learning, and that is the really hard part.

NOTES

1. Dedrick Muhammad, Attieno Davis, Meizhu Lui, and Betsy Leondar-Wright, *The State of the Dream 2004*, January 15, 2004, www.ufenet.org/press/2004/StateoftheDream2004_pr.html.

2. One of the most common fallacies that people fall into is inferring causality from mere correlations. It is quite possible for two things to be positively correlated without there being any cause-and-effect relationship between them. For example, the distance between the Earth's continents is strongly correlated with the number of people on Earth (both are increasing steadily), but there is no causal connection between the two. The correlation exists simply because both quantities have increased with time. But if we managed to reduce the size of the population, continental drift would not reverse direction. Nor would we expect to be able to curb population growth by trying to reverse the direction of continental drift. Before we can infer causation, we have to have at least a plausible model of causation and to test the model in some way.

3. Meredith Phillips et al., "Family Background, Parenting Practices, and the Black–White Test Score Gap," in *The Black–White Test Score Gap*, ed. Christopher Jencks and Meredith Phillips (Washington, DC: Brookings Institution Press, 1998), 103–45.

4. Phillips et al., "Family Background," 103–45.

5. Jencks and Phillips, *The Black–White Test Score Gap*, 23.

6. Jencks and Phillips, *The Black–White Test Score Gap*, 9.

7. Clifford Adelman, *Answers in the Tool Box: Academic Intensity, Attendance Patterns, and Bachelor's Degree Attainment* (Washington, DC: U.S. Department of Education, 1999).

8. David Cay Johnson, *Perfectly Legal* (New York: Portfolio, 2003), 18–19.

6

OTHER POSSIBLE CAUSES
OF THE GAP

If the biological (or genetic) and socioeconomic models do not explain the achievement gap, then that leaves us with a grab bag of various sociological explanations that can be suggested as causes. Almost all of them were raised during the community meeting described in chapter 3 and will be examined more closely in this chapter.

Some of these explanations focus on aspects of black culture that are presumed to be having a negative effect on achievement (and hence are elements of the sociopathological model), while others point to demographic disparities based on ethnicity. But, as with biological and socioeconomic explanations, under close scrutiny even these explanations fail in their task of completely explaining the gap. We have seen, for example, that when it comes to average expenditure per pupil, there is little difference (based on ethnicity) in how much is spent on children.[1]

But it is possible that the *average* expenditure number is not the best measure of educational quality or resources since it is well known that the use of average values can disguise huge variations and highly skewed distributions of resources. Consider, for example, the obvious fact that America is still a very segregated country in terms of where people live. It seems plausible that this could be a cause for the gap, in that black children might be attending schools that are significantly different from those attended by white students, in ways that are not shown in survey data that report averages. But the test-score gap shrinks only by a little even when black and white children attend the *same* schools. Black third graders in predominantly white schools read better than initially similar blacks in predominantly black schools. "But large black–white differences persist even in desegregated schools, and a school's racial mix does not seem to have much effect on changes in reading scores after sixth grade or on math scores at any age."[2]

Another plausible explanation that is very widely and strongly held by parents and teachers is that, for a variety of reasons, black-student culture is averse to high academic achievement, and this negative peer pressure against academic success has a strong influence in damping down black-student academic interest and ambition and thus lowers performance. But some studies suggest that the social costs and benefits of academic success are about the same for blacks and whites, thus casting doubt on this theory.[3]

In terms of work ethic, it is found that both black and white students do little homework outside of school. The median amount of homework hours works out to two to four hours per week for both black and white students, while only 14 percent of whites and 10 percent of blacks do 10 or more hours per week. These are hardly major differences. Also, racial differences are negligible for skipping school.[4] It is true that such sociological studies depend to a large extent on self-reporting by students and are thus difficult to carry out with high accuracy. While the validity of these studies can be challenged on such grounds, it is clear that none of these popular notions is self-evidently true.

Family factors are also frequently pointed out as possible culprits. It is alleged that the traditional model of a stable two-parent family has broken down considerably, especially in the black community. It is argued that many black children live with single parents or with a parent and grandparent, usually female, and that this nontraditional household might lead to lower achievement. But again, some studies show that coming from an intact family has the same effect on test scores as living with a single mother, when the mother's family background, educational attainment, and test scores are held constant.[5] Some caution should be used in interpreting this particular result. What it means is that the marital status of the mother, *by itself*, has little direct effect on student achievement. But it does not say that there could not be secondary effects, in that single mothers may be more likely to have lower levels of educational attainment and test scores and different family and educational backgrounds. These factors could depress their children's achievement to some extent, as can be seen in the discussion in the previous chapter of the effects of socioeconomic status.

One interesting finding (which seems to go against popular stereotypes) is that black parents are more supportive of the idea that their children should strive for higher-level classes in mathematics even if it means lower grades, while white parents feel that their children should stay in the top classes only if they are likely to do well. From an educational standpoint, this attitude of black parents is to be highly commended. Children should be encouraged to seek intellectual challenges and not play it safe. Teachers everywhere bemoan the fact that so many students only seem to want to do the minimum work required to get by, and this support from black parents for more challenging coursework is to be welcomed. But it is not hard to see how, in a perverse way, even this positive attitude has the unintended consequence of *increasing* the grade gap, since it means that white students gravitate toward those courses in which they are assured high grades, while black students do not.

Other popular notions for the achievement gap also wither under close scrutiny. For example, consider the argument that standardized tests are culturally biased against black students. There is no doubt that early versions of standardized tests (such as the SAT), which were aimed at elite college-bound students, had class-based biases that worked against poor students, and this necessarily had a disproportionately negative impact on black students. But the most overt forms of this bias have disappeared as educational access has widened and more students have started taking these tests.

This does not mean that all bias has been eliminated.[6] But there is counterevidence that this cannot be the main cause of the gap. For example, if the SAT was severely biased against black students, you would expect that a black student would have to be academically superior to a white student who had the *same* SAT score and that this would show up in higher grades in college. But black students earn lower college grades than whites with the same SAT scores.[7] (This could still happen if college instructors also had a bias against black students when assigning grades, but I know of no studies that support such a view of *systematic* discrimination.)

The highly charged issues of tracking and leveling in the K–12 sector are somewhat less understood. Ability grouping in early grades has largely symbolic value as a means of placating ambitious parents who like to think of their children as "gifted." But Ronald Ferguson argues that the effect of ability grouping on test performance is not well understood.[8] And even if it were found to have a major influence, it is not clear what one should do in response. "Ferguson's review suggests that the struggle over ability grouping at the elementary level is largely symbolic. Eliminating such classes would not do black children much good, and it would not do whites much harm either. At the secondary level, eliminating demanding courses seems ridiculous. We should be trying to get more black students to take such classes, not trying to eliminate them as an option for whites, who will respond by sending their children elsewhere."[9]

Another suggestion is that the lack of sufficient numbers of black teachers is a cause of black underachievement. This argument seems to rest on assumptions that black teachers better understand black students' needs, are less likely to have negative stereotypes, and are more likely to be role models for black students. But studies suggest that the race of a teacher has little effect on student performance.[10]

Reducing class sizes, while good as a general policy, does not by itself result in closing the gap either. Reducing class sizes from 23 to 15 in K–3 grades raised reading and mathematics scores by only one-third standard deviation for blacks and one-sixth standard deviation for whites. The effect is even smaller in higher grades.[11] But note that the improvement, while small, is still greater for black students than for whites. This is one example of the noteworthy feature that improvements in teaching practices tend to have a disproportionately positive impact on black students, and this will be emphasized repeatedly in this book when we look at strategies for closing the gap.

But there are other, deeper and subtler, sociological reasons that might contribute to the gap but that are not often raised in discussions of the topic in the popular press or other informal settings.

Researcher Signithia Fordham, following up on her research with John Ogbu, looked at the behavior of black high school students in

Washington, D.C., and her study provides one plausible explanation for what keeps black student achievement down and frustrates teachers and black parents alike.[12] She found that there was a marked difference in attitudes toward academic and career success between the generation of blacks that came of age during the civil rights struggle, and their children. This difference, when unrecognized, leads to intense frustration for black parents who cannot understand why their children are not taking advantage of the opportunities their parents struggled and sacrificed to obtain for them. Hence the reasons for this difference in attitudes are important to appreciate.

For the parents, the success of any one black person in any new field was perceived as a vicarious victory for the whole black community because that individual was opening doors that had been hitherto closed to blacks. Other blacks could then emulate the example of the pioneer and follow in his or her footsteps. Thus it was hoped that eventually the community as a whole could pull itself out of the adverse conditions that had resulted from slavery. So the black community rejoiced when Thurgood Marshall became a Supreme Court justice, when Ralph Bunche became an undersecretary general of the United Nations and a Nobel Prize winner, when Althea Gibson and Arthur Ashe became tennis champions, and when others became lawyers, doctors, nurses, college professors, and other kinds of professionals and administrators. It seemed to be only a matter of time before the black community as a whole obtained their fair share of the American dream, which had long been denied them.

But Fordham found that young black people now see things quite differently, and their view does not have this element of hope. What they have observed is that the success of the pioneers did not breed widespread success. A few more blacks made it into the professions, but in nowhere near the numbers necessary to lift up the whole community. Fordham reports that young people see the strategy of individual success leading to community success as a fatally flawed one. They have replaced it with a largely unarticulated, but nevertheless powerfully cohesive, strategy. This has as its premise the idea that the only way the black community as a whole will advance is if all its members stick together and advance together. This way they can keep their ethnic identity intact (i.e., not have to "act white") and demand that society change so that black success can be achieved on its own terms. In carrying out such a strategy, the attempt by any individual black to achieve academic success is seen as a betrayal because it would involve eventually conforming to the norms of white behavior and attitudes. (Recall the impassioned comments by the black student at the community meeting described in chapter 3.)

This causes immense problems for those black students who have higher academic aspirations. Many are torn between wanting to achieve academic success because of their parents' expectations and sacrifices on their behalf, and the natural desire to keep in step with their peers and retain important adolescent friendships. Many of them adopt a middle road, keeping their grades just high enough to avoid trouble at home and preserve good relations with their teachers, but no more. Fordham calls their strategy "racelessness," behaving in what they see as a race-neutral manner so as not to draw attention to themselves. They also tend to study alone and in secret so that they cannot be accused of breaking ranks with their peers. As we will see later, this pattern of isolated study leads to lowered performance when these same students confront the more challenging college environment.

I have sat in on discussions and watched young black high-achieving students squirm when well-meaning whites, trying to discover the magic formula that transforms some black students into high achievers, ask them what it is about them that makes them "different" from the others. These black students don't *want* to be considered different from their peers. They see it as being almost traitorous. They have paid a high personal and social price to pursue their academic success, and any indication that they are thus different from other blacks is painful to them.

We said earlier that the social costs and benefits of academic success are approximately the same for both black and white students, and Ogbu's and Fordham's work may seem at first to contradict that. But this may be because we are talking about two different things. The peculiar form of anti-intellectualism that results in academically minded, high-achieving students being stereotyped as loners, misfits, social outcasts, nerds, and geeks may well be uniformly applied to all ethnic groups. But the perception of ethnic betrayal hinted at by Fordham, while also a form of negative peer pressure, is different from the more common forms and seems to be restricted to the black-student community. One does not hear of corresponding white, Hispanic, or Asian students being similarly accused of somehow losing their ethnic identity simply because of their success in school.

By itself, Fordham's explanation of why black students underperform may not be sufficiently compelling. But Claude Steele of Stanford University (along with Joshua Aronson) has done research indicating the presence of other complementary factors that contribute to poor academic performance by blacks. Steele's and Aronson's research on college students at Stanford and the University of Michigan indicates that when students are placed in a situation in which poor performance on a test would support a stereotype of the inferior abilities of the students' ethnicity or gender, their performance suffers compared with students who do not labor under this preconception.[13] They call this phenomenon "stereotype threat."

For example, when black and white students were given tests that they were told measured their academic abilities, black students did worse than whites. But when matched control groups of black and white students were given the *same* test but were told that the test did not have any such significance but was merely a laboratory tool, the difference in performance disappeared.

What is interesting about Steele's research on stereotype threats is that it is a more general phenomenon than just black–white comparisons. The same thing occurred with men and women. Women's performance deteriorated when they were told that the standardized mathematics test they were taking had shown gender differences, whereas the male–female difference disappeared in the control group when the women were told that the (identical) test had not shown any gender differences. The white men, who were outperforming black and women students, were themselves not immune to the stereotype threat. When they were told that the same tests were being used to compare their abilities with Asians (who are stereotyped as high academic achievers), their performance deteriorated.

Another interesting fact that Steele uncovered is that the "threat" of stereotyping that depresses performance does not have to be overt or very obvious. Just being required to check off their gender or ethnicity on the answer sheet was sufficient to trigger the weaker performance by the students. Steele concludes that the fear that a poor test performance will confirm a stereotype in the mind of an examiner imposes an anxiety on the test taker that is difficult to overcome in the test-taking situation. Given the widespread suspicion that blacks cannot succeed as well as whites in the academic world, or that women are not good at mathematics, both of these groups enter any test-taking situation with a disadvantage compared to those who do not have this fear. Steele suggests that it is this fear that causes these groups to disinvest in education, to assert that it is not important and that they are not going to expend any effort on mastering it. That way, a poor performance is only a measure of the individual's lack of interest in the subject, not a sign of his or her inability to master it.

John Ogbu's studies of minority–dominant relationships in academic performance are more complex.[14] He (and others) has studied the performance of different ethnic-minority groups in the same society (such as African-Americans, Hispanics, Asians, and Native Americans in the United States) and the same ethnic-minority groups in different societies (such as Koreans in Japan and the United States).

The results indicate that the performance of any given minority depends on a complex interplay of factors, such as whether the minority is a voluntary one (as is the case with Asians now and earlier generations of Jewish, Irish, and German immigrants) or an involuntary one (such as blacks due to enslavement, Hispanics due to conquest, and Native Americans due to colonization), and what the perceptions of the dominant community are toward the minority. For example, Koreans and the Buraku (a tribe in Japan that is ethnically identical with other Japanese) do poorly in Japanese schools, where both groups are considered to be academically inferior. But members of those same groups excel when they come to the United States, where teachers tend to view any Koreans and Japanese (being Asian) as academic high achievers. After all, most Americans have no idea that there even exists a Japanese subculture called the Buraku.

Ogbu points out the importance to academic performance of the perception of the relationship between effort and reward. Academic success, like success in almost any aspect of life, depends on the amount of work people are willing to expend. Ogbu argues that people are more likely to work harder if they can see a tangible benefit in return and have a realistic expectation of receiving that benefit. In the case of education, this link lies in the belief that greater educational effort leads to better academic credentials, which in turn lead to gainful and more remunerative employment.

(I will argue later that this kind of extrinsic motivation is ultimately of limited value in enhancing learning by students, but here we are looking only at the differences in the way different ethnic groupings view such extrinsic motivators, and not making judgments as to their overall effectiveness.)

This effort–reward scenario lies at the base of the white work ethic and forms an important component of the lectures delivered to blacks by those who adhere to the sociopathological view of underachievement. If only blacks would work harder, such people assert, they would achieve as much as whites. Ogbu points out that for blacks the effort–reward relationship is not at all obvious. For years blacks were denied employment and education commensurate with their efforts. It did not matter how much they valued education or strove to excel academically, higher levels of education and employment were routinely denied them purely on the basis of their ethnicity. Hence it is unreasonable to expect them to see the work–credential–employment linkage applying to them as strongly as whites might.

But it could be argued that this difference in perception is something that will disappear with time (or, as some might argue, should have already disappeared if not for blacks' clinging to their "victim status"). But Ogbu argues that there is a more pernicious effect still at work. He finds that the value of the reward lies very much in the eye of the beholder because this perception is strongly affected by the group with whom one compares oneself. Ogbu argues that members of the voluntary minority (i.e., the immigrant groups against whom blacks are routinely and adversely compared) compare their rewards with those of their peers *whom they left behind in their native country*. So even if they are working in lower-status jobs in the United States than what they left behind to come here, they tend to be earning more than their peers, and they also feel that their children (for whom they made the sacrifice of coming to the United States) will have greater educational opportunities and chances for advancement than the children of their peers back home. Hence they have a strong sense of achievement that makes them strive even harder, and they instill these values in their children.

But blacks (an involuntary minority) have no reference points to groups outside the United States as a basis for comparison. They instead compare their achievement with that of white people (usually suburban, middle-class whites), and they invariably suffer in the comparison. Ogbu says that in his interviews with "successful" blacks (however one measures that), it does not take long for the sentiment to be expressed that, of course, if they had been white, they would have been even more successful, advanced more in their careers, or made more money. So for blacks, the perceived link between effort and reward is far weaker than it is for whites and voluntary minorities, and we should not be too surprised if the weakness of this link manifests itself in a lower commitment to academic effort.

Although gender differences in academic achievement are not the focus of this book, it is interesting to note that there are strong similarities in these two areas of research. In Virginia Valian's study of gender disparities in her book *Why So Slow?*, she points out that men tend to attribute their success to their ability and effort, which gives them a greater sense of effectiveness and control, while women tend to attribute their success (or lack of it) to luck or other external and uncontrollable factors.[15] But Valian points out that there is also a delicate trade-off between ability and effort. It is popularly believed that if one has a lot of innate ability, then one should be able to achieve success with little effort. Conversely, putting in a lot of effort into something may be construed by others as indicating that one has little ability, and this acts as a disincentive to effort.[16] Applying this idea to Steele's stereotype-threat model, it may be that black students do not expend much effort in academics because this might reinforce the stereotypical belief that they lack academic ability.

Ogbu's research on the importance of attitudes in determining academic success is supported by other studies that look at student attitudes toward education and work. In one such study,[17] students were presented with a list of attitudes that reflect mainstream ideology about education and can be called the American dream. These attitude statements assert that "education is the key to success in the future," that "if everyone in America gets a good education, we can end poverty," that "achievement and effort in school lead to job success later on," that "the way for poor people to become middle class is for them to get a good education," that "school success is a clear path to a better life," that "getting a good education is a practical road to success for young black/white men/women like me," that "young black/white men/women like me have a chance of making it if we do well in school," and that "education really pays off in the future for young black/white men/women like me."

What may come as a surprise to many people is that black students express *greater* agreement with these statements than do white students. In other words, all the exhortations that are made to black students about the value of education are not falling on deaf ears. Black students have heard them and noted them. So we cannot assert that it is ignorance of these benefits that causes black students to underachieve.

The bad news is that black students also express greater agreement than whites with attitudes that reflect doubt about whether these ideals are realistic *for them personally*. For example, they also express greater agreement than white students with the following statements: "Based on their experiences, my parents say people like me are not always paid or promoted according to their education," "all I need to learn for my future is to read, write, and make change," "although my parents tell me to get a good education to get a good job, they face barriers to job success," "when our teachers give us homework, my friends never think of doing it," "people in my family haven't been treated fairly at work, no matter how much education they have," and "studying in school rarely pays off later with good jobs."

Ogbu's study of minority underachievement in Shaker Heights reinforces the findings of the above study.[18] When asked what it takes to succeed in school, the black students recited a list of things they needed to do that would make any traditional educator proud: go to class regularly, listen to the teacher, work hard, do the homework, and so on. But when asked if they actually did any of these things, they said they didn't. In other words, they knew what needed to be done to succeed academically, but they did not do it.

Ogbu also found that the children of successful black parents seemed to feel that they too would be successful like their parents without having to do all the hard work they did. They seemed to feel that success would somehow come to them, in some mysterious and unarticulated way. The reasons for this disconnect are not clear. Perhaps among the blacks who came of age during the difficult struggles for civil rights there is a stoicism that prevents them from talking about how hard they had to fight for what they now have, what they had to endure. I am told that the immediate survivors of the Jewish Holocaust did much the same thing with their children, not talking much about what they went through. They may be simply trying not to relive the pain of those days in their own minds or trying to spare their children the pain they themselves went through. But instead they may be giving their children a false sense of what it takes to achieve success.

To summarize, it seems as if black students believe that there exists an educational meritocracy in America but that it does not apply to them. One can hardly be surprised at this cynical attitude. After all, it was only their parents' generation that had the experience of feeling that they could only aspire to low-level clerical jobs in the post office and other government agencies, however good they were academically. Encountering such a pervasive cynicism in their own homes and neighborhoods cannot help but have an adverse impact on student attitudes toward education and school.

It appears that we are in a hopeless situation. It seems that many of the more commonly articulated solutions for solving the achievement gap, especially those that can be fairly easily implemented by legislative or administrative fiats, are unlikely to be successful since the research indicates that these factors cannot completely explain the gap. The more important causes of the gap seem to have deep social and historical roots that make it extremely difficult to devise and implement solutions. But there is hope. The next chapter will highlight some success stories that suggest practical strategies to overcoming the immense barriers that lie in the way of solving the problem of the educational achievement gap.

NOTES

1. Christopher Jencks and Meredith Phillips, eds., *The Black–White Test Score Gap* (Washington, DC: Brookings Institution Press, 1998), 9.

2. Jencks and Phillips, *The Black–White Test Score Gap*, 9.

3. Philip J. Cook and Jens Ludwig, "The Burden of 'Acting White': Do Black Adolescents Disparage Academic Achievement?" in *The Black–White Test Score Gap*, ed. Jencks and Phillips, 375–400.

4. Cook and Ludwig, "The Burden of 'Acting White,'" 375–400.

5. Meredith Phillips et al., "Family Background, Parenting Practices, and the Black–White Test Score Gap," in *The Black–White Test Score Gap*, ed. Jencks and Phillips, 103–45.

6. For examples, see W. James Popham, *The Truth about Testing: An Educator's Call to Action* (Alexandria, VA: ASCD, 2001).

7. Frederick E. Vars and William G. Bowen, "Scholastic Aptitude Test Scores, Race and Academic Performance in Selective Colleges and Universities," in *The Black–White Test Score Gap*, ed. Jencks and Phillips, 457–79; and Thomas J. Kane, "Racial and Ethnic Preferences in College Admissions," in *The Black–White Test Score Gap*, ed. Jencks and Phillips, 431–56.

8. Ronald F. Ferguson, "Can Schools Narrow the Black–White Test Score Gap?" in *The Black–White Test Score Gap*, ed. Jencks and Phillips, 318–74.

9. Jencks and Phillips, *The Black–White Test Score Gap*, 45.

10. Ronald F. Ferguson, "Teachers' Expectations and the Test Score Gap," in *The Black–White Test Score Gap*, ed. Jencks and Phillips, 273–317.

11. Ferguson, "Can Schools Narrow the Black–White Test Score Gap?," 318–74. See also p. 31.

12. Signithia Fordham, "Racelessness as a Factor in Black Students' School Success," *Harvard Educational Review* 58, no.1 (1988): 54–84; Signithia Fordham and John Ogbu, "Black Students' School Success: Coping with the Burden of Acting White," *Urban Review* 18, no. 3 (1986): 176–206.

13. Claude M. Steele and Joshua Aronson, "Stereotype Threat and the Intellectual Test Performance of African Americans," *Journal of Personality and Social Psychology* 95, no. 5 (1995): 797–811; David J. Lewin, "Subtle Clues Elicit Stereotypes' Impact on Black Students," *Journal of NIH Research* (November 1995): 24–26.

14. John U. Ogbu, "Immigrant and Involuntary Minorities in Comparative Perspective," Yongsook Lee, "Koreans in Japan and the United States," and Nobuo K. Shimahara, "Social Mobility and Education: Burakumin in Japan," in *Minority Status and Schooling: A Comparative Study of Immigrant and Involuntary Minorities*, ed. Margaret Gibson and John Ogbu (New York: Garland Science, 1991), 3–33.

15. Virginia Valian, *Why So Slow?: The Advancement of Women* (Cambridge, MA: MIT Press, 1998), chap. 9.

16. Valian, *Why So Slow?*, 185.

17. Ferguson, "Teachers' Expectations," 273–317.

18. John U. Ogbu, *Black American Students in an Affluent Suburb* (Mahwah, NJ: Lawrence Erlbaum, 2003).

7

SUCCESS STORIES AND WHAT WE CAN LEARN FROM THEM

The focus so far has been on identifying the causes of low academic performance of black children. We have seen that they lie in factors rooted deeply in history, intertwined with broad social, economic, and political strands, and the causes cannot be simply swept away by legislative or administrative action, by exhortations, or by identifying and weeding out people with racial prejudice from public life.

The most deeply pessimistic diagnosis of the gap is that it is caused by genetic and evolutionary factors. If true, then the situation is hopeless since there is virtually nothing that can be done about this. There are enough countervailing studies (discussed in chapter 4) to suggest that this explanation of the gap can be dismissed as flatly wrong.

The more optimistic diagnoses of the achievement gap are that it is caused by factors amenable to quick-fix solutions. Some solutions lie within the control of individual families, such as turning off the TV at home, getting parents more involved in their children's schooling, and so on. These are all good suggestions from a general standpoint but are not likely to produce significant reductions in the achievement gap. Diagnoses that suggest fairly straightforward (but politically difficult) solutions in schools (such as hiring more black teachers, eliminating tracking and standardized tests, encouraging teachers to have high expectations of black students, catering to more diverse learning styles) are also not likely to have much beneficial effect and can sometimes even be harmful.

As discussed in previous chapters, the factors that can explain a significant fraction (but not all) of the achievement gap have the negative feature that they do not suggest any specific program of action. Socioeconomic differences, stereotype threats, and the differential effort–reward relationships between the black and white communities all arise from broad, complex, historical, economic, and social forces over which educational systems, local communities, and families have little or no control.

It might seem that the situation is hopeless, that the things we can do have little effect, while the things that have an effect are beyond our control. Does this mean that nothing can be done and that we have to patiently wait for time to change the social climate we live in? This chapter will argue that this is not the case. The good news is that there are specific educational strategies that provide some hope of closing and even eliminating the gap, and it is to these that we now turn.

Mathematics education plays an important role in understanding the causes of the achievement gap. Ever since the former Soviet Union surprised the world by launching the first artificial satellite (*Sputnik I*) into orbit in 1957, the United States has paid close attention to the performance of its students in mathematics and science education, perceiving these two specific areas as the key to achieving technological and military dominance of the world. As a result, mathematics performance has been studied closely and extensively and provides us with a wealth of data on what seems to work and what does not. It is not the purpose of this book to survey that vast literature, but instead we will focus on those aspects that shed some light on the achievement gap.

The Adelman study on the most significant factors that influence the rate at which high school students graduate from college (discussed in chapter 5) showed that within the high school curriculum, the highest level of mathematics taken by students has the strongest influence on degree completion. Finishing a course beyond the level of algebra 2 (for example, taking trigonometry or precalculus) more than doubles the odds that a student who enters college will complete a bachelor's degree.[1]

Why mathematics plays such a crucial role is a little puzzling. Even though mathematics played a major role in my own education and is a subject that I value highly, it is hard for me to argue that mathematics has some intrinsic value in learning not possessed by other subjects. After all, most people manage to live their lives without feeling an urgent need to understand the mysteries of, say, the cosine function or without being able to calculate derivatives and integrals. For most everyday purposes, some facility with basic elements of arithmetic, the ability to interpret graphs and charts, and a rudimentary knowledge of probability and statistics are all that people need to cope with the world around them. It could be argued that government, ethics, health, accounting, and economics provide more immediate and tangible benefits for everyday life than mathematics.

Some might argue that a good mathematics education imparts a kind of mental rigor and teaches the mind certain important logical and analytical skills that transfer to other areas as well, and thus results in enhanced performance in seemingly unrelated subjects. But similar arguments have been made in the past, during the heyday of classical education, for the study of subjects like Latin and Greek. It was felt that the rigor of these subjects disciplined students' minds in a manner that made for superior thinking overall. These arguments are now not seen as very credible, and it may be that current similar claims for mathematics will be similarly discounted in the future.

Adelman's conclusion about the importance of mathematics may be simply due to the fact that mathematics can serve as a proxy measure for overall school quality. In other words, a school that has the ability to provide advanced mathematics courses to most of its students is also probably a school that has in place a lot of the other features that provide a quality education. But whatever might be going on beneath the surface, there is no question that mathematics performance tends to have high predictive power when it comes to determining future academic performance.

But one does not need to reach for such a tenuous benefit from mathematics education. There are also direct and tangible advantages of knowing more mathematics, especially when it comes to college education. Many subjects that formerly were substantially qualitative (biology, psychology, economics, government, geography) are now taking on more quantitative aspects. Lack of comfort with mathematics can make students feel insecure about taking these subjects and thereby undermine their performance, well out of proportion to the actual level or quantity of mathematics involved. For whatever reason, next to reading, mathematics performance has become a key indicator of how well schools are functioning. It also functions as a so-called "gatekeeper" subject, so that success or failure in mathematics can determine what range of options a student has when it comes to further studies.

Mathematics teaching and learning has also been the toughest educational problem, typically having the lowest pass rates in proficiency tests for all ethnic groups. With the rise in the so-called "accountability" movement in education and its emphasis on proficiency tests, trying to improve mathematics performance has been the subject of intense study. As a result, the mathematics-education community has, within the last two decades, made a determined effort to address the problems of mathematics education. Consequently, mathematics education and testing provide us with one of the richest sources of data and analysis.

Since mathematics clearly plays an important role in the future success of students, what it takes to reduce the achievement gap in mathematics might give us insight into how to address the overall achievement gap, and we will now turn to some of the more interesting results of these efforts.

In 1989, the National Council of Teachers of Mathematics (NCTM) issued its *Curriculum and Evaluation Standards for School Mathematics*, interweaving content (number, algebra, geometry, measurement, data analysis, and probability) with process (problem solving, reasoning and proof, connections, communication, and representation). This was a comprehensive document, the result of years of collaboration among mathematicians and educators who tried to identify what mathematics students needed to know at various points in their school careers and how those ideas could best be taught.

The hope was that by having a coherent set of vertically integrated high standards in mathematics for each grade, teachers would be able to avoid the major criticisms that are leveled against mathematics education in the United States, which is that the curriculum is too broad and shallow, with far too many concepts to be mastered each year. The resulting fast-paced instruction resulted in little learning occurring in each grade, leading to repetition of the same material from year to year with no significant advance in learning on the part of students. It was hoped that the new standards-based curricula would enable teachers to avoid this cycle of futility and impart a high-quality education.

Of course high standards alone are not enough, however clearly articulated. Teachers also need correspondingly high-quality curricular materials, and by the mid-nineties, such curricula became available for adoption. Large-scale data are now beginning to come in about the effectiveness of these materials, allowing for analysis of the results of such standards-based education.

A recent study by Alan Schoenfeld points to some significant features that have emerged from this effort.[2] Schoenfeld analyzed the results of mathematics-education reform efforts in the Pittsburgh schools. This system has challenging demographics: 40,000 students in 97 public schools (59 elementary, 19 middle, 11 high, and 8 other); 56 percent black and 44 percent white/other; with more than 60 percent qualifying for free or reduced-price lunches. Most significantly for the purpose of the Schoenfeld study, since the early 1990s, Pittsburgh has made a serious effort to implement standards-based education in mathematics and other subject areas.

In Schoenfeld's analysis, he distinguished between what were called strong-implementation teachers and weak-implementation teachers, and strong-implementation schools and weak-implementation schools.

Strong-implementation teachers were those teachers in whose classrooms students were familiar with activities and procedures specific to the NCTM reform curriculum. Visual aids and manipulative materials appropriate to the curriculum were accessible and showed clear signs of use and were not (as has happened in the past with other reform efforts in mathematics and science) carefully stored away in closets. Also, in these teachers' classrooms, students had frequent opportunities to work together in cooperative groups and explain their work to each other, and student work involved projects and activities that were specific to the reform curriculum. Also, no other curricula were being used, indicating that these teachers were not using the new reform-based curriculum as merely "enrichment" activities to supplement traditional curricula.

Weak-implementation teachers, by contrast, were those teachers who did not meet the above criteria. The Schoenfeld study compared the performance in mathematics of students in what were called strong-implementation schools (i.e., schools in which *all* the teachers were considered strong implementers) with the students in weak-implementation schools (in which at most only one or two teachers were strong implementers).

The results show that use of the reform curricula in the strong-implementation schools significantly narrowed the gap between whites and underrepresented minorities, while increasing the performance of *both* groups in *all* categories. The importance of this last fact cannot be overemphasized. Many people are wary of attempts to close the achievement gap because of fears that this can only be done by "dumbing down" the curriculum so that everyone is equal in their mediocrity. Showing that this need not happen is important if there is to be any chance of persuading the general public that closing the achievement gap is an important goal.

On tests of so-called "basic skills" in mathematics (the skills championed so vociferously by accountability advocates), white-student performance increased from 48 percent to 72 percent (a 50 percent increase), while blacks increased from 30 percent to 75 percent (a 150 percent increase). This is an important result. Following the alleged fiasco of the "new math" reforms that followed the *Sputnik* revolution, many people are leery of mathematics-reform curricula because they feel that these innovations result in lower levels of skills in "basic" mathematics, manifested in the ability to correctly add, subtract, multiply, and divide without utilizing calculators and using the usual base-10 number system. Such people tend to repeat the mantra that these "basics" must be taught first (using heavy doses of drill) before more complex ideas (such as arithmetic using base numbers other than 10) and higher-level thinking skills are attempted.

In reality, though, there is no clear hierarchy of learning, and there is no neutral way of learning basic skills. It can be done in such a way (such as repeated drilling and mindless memorization) that results in lower abilities to process higher-level knowledge, or learned in a way (using inquiry-based methods) that enhances them. As we will see later, these differences in the way so-called basic skills are taught has important consequences for the achievement gap.

Going back to the Schoenfeld study of Pittsburgh schools, on problem-solving skills, whites increased from 18 percent to 54 percent (a 200 percent increase), while black performance went from 4 percent to 32 per-

cent (a 700 percent increase). On mathematics concepts, whites increased from 20 percent to 60 percent (a 200 percent increase), while
black performance increased from 4 percent to 40 percent (a 900 percent
increase). Thus, *while both groups improve, the minority groups improve
by much greater amounts.* This last point is extremely important when
we look later at the political challenges that must inevitably be faced
when trying to implement any changes that have an impact on the
achievement gap.

What these data suggest is that it is possible to greatly reduce (and in
some areas eliminate) the gap in mathematics achievement by adopting
educational measures that *are not directly targeting the achievement
gap or specific minority groups.* The educational remedies adopted
were not ethnicity-specific. The reductions in gaps were achieved by a
general focus on improving the educational achievement of *all* students,
whatever their ethnicity, gender, or socioeconomic status.

That such a broader effort at improvement is both necessary and desirable can be seen by looking at the National Assessment of Educational Progress results for mathematics. These NAEP assessments (popularly referred to as "the nation's report card") are periodically given to
a representative cross section of students across the country at various
grade levels and are graded on a 0 to 500 scale. Since these assessments
take a randomized sample of students, the results are a more accurate
measure of student achievement than those for self-selected groups like
SAT takers.

The NAEP mathematics results for grade 12 students in 2000 had the
average white score at 308 and the average black score at 274.[3] A traditional focus on eliminating the gap would try and find ways to raise black
scores to about 308, thus eliminating the 34-point gap. But even if we
could achieve this, would the underlying problem have been solved?

I have suggested that the gap we should be focusing on is the difference between where all students are now and where they should be.
The NAEP scores allow us to make this comparison because benchmark
levels are specified, enabling one to make judgments about the levels
reached by students. The reality is quite depressing. For grade 12 students, a basic level of achievement in mathematics (denoting partial
mastery of knowledge and skills that are fundamental for proficient
work) requires a minimum score of 288; a proficient level (representing

solid academic performance and competency over challenging subject matter) requires 336; the advanced level (representing superior performance) requires a minimum score of 367.

NAEP believes that all students should reach at least the proficient level score of 336. Thus we see that the average scores of *both* ethnic groups are well below proficient. In fact only 20 percent of whites score above proficient levels, while only 3 percent of blacks are above proficient. So even if, after tremendous efforts, we were to raise black scores to the white score level of 308, both communities would still have about 80 percent of students below proficiency levels. In other words, they would be equal, but equally dismal. There is little point in eliminating the achievement gap in this way. It may solve the political problem of inequality, but it would not solve the educational problem of mass student underachievement. Ignoring the fact that large numbers of white students are also being left behind academically prevents us from seeing that there is a deeper underlying problem in education.

What would it take to achieve the more worthwhile goal of having all students reach at least the proficiency level of 336? The Schoenfeld analysis of the Pittsburgh schools indicates that it takes an effort to provide all-around good teaching. It took about *10 years* of support and professional development (collaborative study, observation, curricular knowledge, and lesson refinement as part of the teachers' ongoing *daily* responsibilities) for even talented beginning teachers to acquire the characteristics of strong-implementation teachers, that is, to become accomplished professionals. (It is interesting that this particular result is replicated in independent studies of college teachers as well.[4]) This rarely happens in our school systems. New teachers are unceremoniously dumped into classrooms and left to fend for themselves as best as they can. Is it any wonder that so many novice teachers fail to develop as hoped, and even leave teaching, though they may have shown promise at the beginning?

Another interesting study that again focuses on mathematics originated around 1974 at the University of California at Berkeley and was the result of an observation by mathematics instructor Uri Treisman.[5] He noticed (as had countless other college instructors before him) that black and Hispanic students were failing the introductory mathematics courses in far greater numbers than any other ethnic group and were thus more likely to drop out of college. This occurred despite remedial courses, interventions, and such aimed directly at these at-risk groups.

He inquired among his colleagues as to the possible reasons for this phenomenon and was given the usual list of suspect causes: Black students tend to come from homes in which there is more poverty, less stability, and lack of emphasis on education. They went to poorer high schools and were thus less prepared, lacked motivation, and so forth. Treisman, rather than unquestioningly accepting these typical coffee-room boilerplate diagnoses, actually investigated to see if they were true. What he found was that in actual fact the black students at Berkeley came from families in which there was an intense emphasis on education and high levels of parental pride and support for their children's going to college, and that many had gone to excellent high schools and were as well prepared as any other group. There was also a wide diversity within them, some coming from integrated middle-class suburban neighborhoods, others from inner-city segregated ones. Clearly the conventional wisdom did not hold, and the causes of their poor achievement lay elsewhere.

What Treisman then did was narrow his investigation to just two groups—blacks and the high-achieving ethnic Chinese minority. He studied all aspects of the two groups' lives (going to the extent of even living with them) to see what factors might be contributing to their hugely different performances, and what he found was interesting. He discovered that while both groups had social interactions within their own groups, the Chinese students also *studied* together, routinely analyzing lectures and instructors, sharing tips and explanations and strategies for success. They had an enormously efficient information network for sharing what worked and what didn't. If someone made a mistake in some course, others quickly learned of it and did not repeat it.

In contrast, the black students socialized together just like the Chinese but then went their separate ways for studying, perhaps as a result of the habits acquired due to the high school experiences described by Signithia Fordham (and which were discussed in chapter 6). This resulted in a much slower pace of learning, with the black students learning from their mistakes the hard way by actually making those mistakes themselves. Black students also typically had no idea where they stood with respect to the rest of the class, and they were usually surprised by the fact that they received poor grades despite doing exactly what they thought was expected of them, such as going to class, handing in all their assignments on time, and studying for as many hours as other students.

Treisman addressed this problem in his own classes by creating a workshop model for his mathematics students. In these workshops, students were placed in groups and worked on mathematics problems collaboratively. Discussion and the sharing of information was actively encouraged and rewarded. By this means, Treisman sought to inculcate the value of group academic effort and sharing in the minds of *all* his students, not just those who happened to chance upon this effective strategy for achieving academic success.

Another notable feature of this experiment was that the working groups were mixed ethnically and in terms of prior achievement. A third noteworthy feature was that the students were given *very challenging* problems to work on, much harder than the ones they would normally have encountered in their regular courses.

It is interesting that these innovations, although they preceded Claude Steele's research, have the kinds of features that avoid triggering the stereotype threat identified by him. The ethnically mixed nature of the groups avoids the perception that this was a remedial program aimed at blacks, while the explicitly challenging nature of the problems posed to the students meant that there was no stigma attached to failing to solve them. Failure was considered to be due to the problems' being hard, not because a student was of a certain ethnicity and hence not capable of achieving academic success. In addition, when students did succeed in solving a problem, they experienced a sense of exhilaration and power at having achieved mastery of something *difficult*, which, as anyone who has experienced it will testify, is the only real and lasting incentive for striving toward high achievement. What Treisman found was that as a result of his workshop model, black students' performance improved by as much as one letter grade.

Subsequent research supports the effectiveness of Treisman's strategy. Claude Steele has also initiated a program at the University of Michigan, which uses the same idea of mixed groups of students working on challenging tasks.[6] The program's director reports that positive results are observed for all students in the program, regardless of race.

Ellis Cose, in his book *Color-Blind*, describes another success story of black education, this time at Xavier University, a historically black college in New Orleans.[7] This university took to heart the message of psychometrician Arthur Whimbey, who in his book *Intelligence Can Be Taught* argued that students can be taught to perform better academically by a suitably planned program that stresses the importance of higher-level thinking skills.[8] By using a Whimbey-inspired curriculum, incoming freshmen so improved their academic performance that now Xavier is the single biggest supplier of black graduates to medical schools, despite its relatively small enrollment. Once again it must be emphasized that what was stressed in this program was the challenging nature of the academic program, the drive for *excellence* as opposed to remediation.

Many efforts at closing the achievement gap tend toward the creation of remedial programs. Traditional remedial courses designed for underachieving students are largely based on the assumption that poor performance is due to lack of adequate preparation, that weaker students are handicapped due to a lack of so-called basic skills and knowledge. Hence these courses tend to have a strong emphasis on drilling students on these so-called basics.

But what such courses neglect to adequately take into account is that students fall behind academically for a variety of reasons, not the least of which is that they have not mastered the *higher*-level knowledge-acquisition, reasoning, and problem-solving skills that are the prerequisites for success in real life. So even if students are drilled in the "basics" so that they reach the same hypothetical starting line as others, they start falling behind again as soon as they encounter *new* material, because they do not know how to process the new information most efficiently. And it is of little use to try to overcome this problem by adding specialized courses on "critical thinking" or "problem solving." High-level thinking skills become ingrained in an individual only if he or she is given repeated opportunities to practice those skills in the context of learning a diverse set of subject-matter content. They cannot be acquired by means of stand-alone courses devoid of meaningful and useful content.

Even worse, the drill methods often used in remedial courses bore the students (thus turning them off education even more) and tend to reinforce the *low*-level thinking skills that caused them to fall behind in the first place, at the expense of the higher-level ones, thus compounding the problem instead of solving it. On the other hand, if students are given interesting and challenging problems to work on, things that pique their interest and are relevant to their lives, they are more likely to acquire the so-called basic skills as a means to solving the problems of real interest, not as an end in itself.

Treisman's work also sheds light on the role that self-esteem plays in student achievement. There is no question that achieving success at some task can be a great motivator for further effort. The importance of having a sense of self-efficacy cannot be underestimated. But this self-esteem idea has become hopelessly misapplied by thinking that what is needed is to enable underachieving students to experience *any* kind of success so that they will improve their self-esteem. This has led to attempts by some teachers to make the bar for success very low for their students, in the hope that students will achieve success and thus get enthused about learning.

Such an approach can have negative effects. Students need appropriate and meaningful challenges. But a report by the Educational Trust asserts that very little is expected from students in high-poverty classrooms. Those students get few assignments, and even those are of low quality. Even in high school, these students are asked to color and draw pictures as writing assignments. They are given As for work that would merit Cs and Ds elsewhere, all in a misguided effort to improve their self-esteem.[9]

In the course of my work with professional-development programs, an earnest and well-meaning teacher once told me of her frustration with attempts to improve students' self-esteem in her exclusively black school district. After teaching a section of the mathematics course, she would give her students a practice test. She would then grade the tests and hand them back to the students, along with the answer key, and discuss the test. The "real" test, which was exactly the same as the practice test, was then given, with the students being aware beforehand that the real test was going to be the same as the practice test. The teacher told me that she adopted this strategy so that the students would score well on the test and thus experience a boost in their self-esteem. Yet the teacher complained that the students still did badly on the test, and this was disappointing to her.

It is not hard to understand why the students were not putting in any effort to just memorize the answers to the practice test and reproduce them on the real test. It was because the "real" test was not a real test of anything meaningful. The task was so trivially simple as to be humiliating. Being forced to do something trivial is insulting. As an example, suppose someone in authority over you demands that you answer what seems to be an extremely easy question. If you answer it correctly, all it demonstrates is your obsequiousness to authority, your willingness to jump through hoops set by others. If you answer and get it wrong, that marks you as an incredibly stupid person. There is no way to answer so that you can feel good about yourself. So the one response that at least partially maintains your pride is to shrug off the assignment, to try and devalue or dismiss it, and to treat it as not worth doing. This is an instinctive response that children, and even adults, have to such insulting assignments.

To illustrate that it is not just children who react in this way, Virginia Valian, in her study of gender differences referred to in the previous chapter, tells an anecdote[10] in which a physician, Dr. X, asks a group of people going to a medical conference whether anyone has a copy of that day's *New York Times* because he likes to do the daily crossword puzzle and has forgotten to bring his own paper. Managing to obtain that day's puzzle, he announces that he does it every morning and brags about always starting at the top and working his way down. (Crossword-puzzle aficionados know that doing it this way is harder and shows superior skill compared to doing the easier clues first and using the results to figure out the harder clues.)

Valian says to the group in Dr. X's presence that she has done the puzzle already and that "it's a bit too easy today." She observes that she has immediately placed Dr. X in a quandary. "By labeling the puzzle easy, I have reduced the explanations at his disposal. Should he succeed, he cannot attribute his success to his ability. Should he fail, he cannot attribute his failure to difficulty or bad luck." But Dr. X, after being momentarily taken aback, recovers and says, " I can always tell how tired I am by whether or not I finish." Thus, although he still cannot take credit if he succeeds, he has avoided blame if he fails, since the failure has been attributed to tiredness and not lack of ability.

As the Treisman study indicated, students respond well to *real* challenges because then failure is perceived as being due to the challenging nature of the task, not due to any intrinsic inability. People respond well to challenges that are slightly beyond their grasp because success brings with it a pleasurable sense of accomplishment. If you look at what children and adults do for recreation, they instinctively gravitate toward, or set for themselves, tasks that stretch their abilities. This is true for puzzles (people select crossword puzzles that are not too hard or too easy), basketball (players at practice tend to set themselves realistic but not easy goals), or computer games. Manufacturers of such games have long realized this and design them to have a choice of different challenge levels so that players can slowly work themselves up to higher and higher levels of proficiency.

Why can't we learn to do the same things in education? After all, looked at dispassionately, there is no intrinsic value in doing a crossword puzzle, throwing a ball through a hoop, or pushing knobs on a game control and destroying some computer-generated villain. Yet people will spend enormous amounts of their spare time trying to improve their skill at these things. What is the essential difference between such activities and doing an integral in calculus or solving a physics problem or analyzing the motivations and actions of the principal characters in *Hamlet*? I argue that there is no essential difference in the intrinsic nature of the task itself. What is significant is the attitude that is brought to the task, which is largely determined by the environment in which the task is performed.

Clearly people prefer to do things for a lot of reasons that have nothing to do with the intrinsic merit of the activity or even its financial reward. People tend to prefer things where they have choice over what they do, how much time they devote to it, their perception of the degree of challenge, and the amount of support and guidance they receive. We may not be able to completely replicate all these conditions in the classroom, but with some imagination and a different perspective on learning, we should be able to do a lot more than we are doing now. At present, classrooms are places where students feel they give up all freedoms as soon as they walk through the door. It does not have to be that way. We need to learn from what makes students motivated to do things when they are on their own, and apply those lessons in teaching.

In examining all these success stories, two significant features stand out. The methods used were race-neutral, and the strategies were aimed at high-level cognitive tasks, not at low-level remedial work. The next chapter will look more closely at the implications of these results.

NOTES

1. Clifford Adelman, *Answers in the Tool Box: Academic Intensity, Attendance Patterns, and Bachelor's Degree Attainment* (U.S. Department of Education, 1999).

2. Alan H. Schoenfeld, "Making Mathematics Work for All Children: Issues of Standards, Testing, and Equity," *Educational Researcher* 31, no. 1 (January/February 2002): 13–25.

3. National Center for Educational Statistics (NCES) 2001-517, "The Nation's Report Card: Mathematics 2000," U.S. Department of Education, Office of Educational Research and Improvement, August 2001.

4. Robert Boice, *Advice for New Faculty Members: Nihil Nimus* (Boston: Allyn and Bacon, 2000).

5. Uri Treisman, "Studying Students Studying Calculus: A Look at the Lives of Minority Students in College," *The College Mathematics Journal* 23, no. 5 (November 1992): 362–72.

6. Claude M. Steele, "Black Students Live Down to Expectations," *New York Times*, 3 August 1995.

7. Ellis Cose, *Color-Blind: Seeing beyond Race in a Race-Obsessed World* (New York: Perennial, 1998).

8. Arthur Whimbey and Linda Shaw Whimbey, *Intelligence Can Be Taught* (New York: Dutton, 1980).

9. Kati Haycock, Craig Jerald, and Sandra Huang, "Closing the Gap: Done in a Decade," *Education Trust: Thinking K–16* 5, no. 2 (Spring 2001): 3; Kati Haycock, "Closing the Achievement Gap," *Educational Leadership* (March 2001): 6–11.

10. Virginia Valian, *Why So Slow?: The Advancement of Women* (Cambridge, MA: MIT Press, 1998), 175.

8

WHY GOOD TEACHING MATTERS AND WHAT IT TAKES TO ACHIEVE IT

Good teaching is important for learning. Students who have the good fortune to have excellent teachers learn more than students who have poor teachers. These statements seem so obvious that it seems hardly worthwhile to state them. But buried in them are deep subtleties that will be explored in this chapter: What exactly makes a good teacher? What constitutes good teaching? What does it take to achieve both?

For the purposes of this book, the important role that good teaching plays in closing the achievement gap needs to be particularly emphasized. After all, if good teaching, like a rising tide lifting all boats, increased the performance of all students by similar amounts, that would be a good thing, but the gap would still remain. What will be argued is that good teaching is a tide that lifts all boats by *unequal* amounts. It has a disproportionately positive effect on underachieving groups, thus closing the gap.

One indicator of why this happens can be found in studies that show that the impact of teacher expectations is *two to three times* as much for black students as for whites (and also larger for girls and for low-income families). For 81 percent of black females and 62 percent of black males, pleasing the teacher is more important than pleasing the parent, compared with only 28 percent of white females and 32 percent of white males.[1] In other words, the impact of the teacher on the student is far greater for minority students. Since effective teachers produce as much as six times the learning gains produced by the least effective teachers,[2] it should not be surprising that good teachers can produce a differentially positive effect on minority students.

The negative implications of these same data are that poor teaching also has a disproportionately deleterious effect on black students, driving down their learning more than it does for white students. The importance of this is not fully appreciated by teachers. I have encountered many well-intentioned teachers who pride themselves on their toughness. They recognize that while they may be hard on their students, they take refuge in the fact that they are "fair," in that they treat everyone equally harshly. These teachers probably think that their students may not like or appreciate their actions now but will understand and thank them in the future. An article in the Cleveland daily newspaper describes a teacher who believes in this kind of philosophy and says that she does not care if her students like her or not, but only that they learn.[3]

But the fact that you treat everyone equally does not mean that the effects of that treatment are the same for everyone. I have met successful academics who have said that the scorn and ridicule they received from a teacher inspired them to work hard and excel just so they could prove that person wrong. In these cases, the teachers' dismissive attitude seemed to act as a spur for the students to aim higher. But for others, who may not have started out with the same sense of self-assurance, such harsh treatment from the teacher may persuade them that they should not continue to study in that discipline, that they do not belong, and it may thus lead to lower performance. So it is not sufficient that we teach and treat all students equally; we should teach all students equally and *well*.

The main thesis of this book is that good teaching is what we need to focus on if we wish to make progress in closing the gap. Such an approach hints at an educational strategy that everyone, of any ethnicity, can embrace and that can overcome the forces that create disparities in achievement. But in order to get there, we have to dispel some of the other myths that surround the role of teachers and the achievement gap.

THE IMPORTANCE OF TEACHER EXPECTATIONS

The frequently raised charge that teachers have lower expectations for black students than for white students turns out to have some support.[4] Since the teaching profession is predominantly white, it is tempting to infer that this phenomenon is caused by simple racism, or that the solution lies in changing the teachers. But the situation is more complex than that.

For one thing, it is interesting that the race of a teacher has little effect on student performance.[5] So the often-suggested solution that this particular problem will go away if significantly larger numbers of black teachers are hired is not likely to work. Hiring more black teachers may well be a good idea in terms of furthering worthwhile goals of employment equity, but we should not be sanguine that it will make a big dent in the problem of the achievement gap.

It turns out that the reason for the lower expectations is because black students' past performance and behavior are believed to have been worse than that of whites.[6] Teachers live in the same universe that the rest of us do and are subject to the same impressions conveyed by newspapers, television, radio, and the Internet. They know, just like everyone else, that black students underperform academically and that they get into trouble with school authorities and the law at greater rates than white students. However much an individual teacher might resist racist thinking and wish to believe that everyone is equal, it should not be surprising that when confronted with an unknown black child, they assume that the child will be "typical" and thus expect less from that child.

The good news is that there is little evidence that teachers' lower expectations of black students are based simply on color. Teacher expectations do not differ by race when asked to assess children whom they know have performed equally well and have behaved equally well in the past based on previous grades and test scores, self-perception of mathematics ability, and self-reported levels of effort and time spent on homework.[7] In other words, if teachers have equal knowledge of individual students, their expectations are not influenced by a student's color. So the problem of teacher expectations differing for black and white students is not simply one of racial prejudice.

But the reality of lower expectations of black students, however benign its cause, has as adverse an impact on the achievement gap as if it were due to malice or ignorance. By basing their expectations on beliefs about children's past performance and behavior, teachers perpetuate racial disparities in achievement. For example, teachers can learn enough about children in the first few weeks of first grade to predict accurately their rank order on examinations held at the beginning of the second year.[8] Like the rest of us, teachers find it hard to overcome their first impressions of someone. Once set, teacher expectations do not change much, and it is plausible that teacher expectations are more rigid for blacks, women, and low-income students than for others.

Given that teacher expectations of students are grounded in broad, socially based reasons, simply exhorting teachers to have more faith in black children's potential is unlikely to change expectations. It is as futile as exhorting students to study more because it is good for them. Teachers, like students, know what they *should* believe and what they *should* do. The question is how to translate this intellectual knowledge into concrete actions. Teachers, if they are to overcome their prior conception of black students, need professional-development programs in which they can actually see for themselves disadvantaged black children performing at high levels.[9]

As can be seen by the example of the strong-implementation teachers in the Pittsburgh schools discussed in chapter 7, having "good" teachers in the classroom is the key to solving the problem of the achievement gap. But how you define good teaching depends on what you view the act of teaching to be. Before we address the question of what good teaching consists of, it is useful to see what it is *not*. One thing that it definitely is not is a specific set of teaching practices. There is no single good way of teaching. Over the years, hosts of teaching innovations have entered educational practice under a variety of names: inquiry-based learning, constructivism, collaborative learning, active learning, and so on. All of these philosophies and techniques are of value, but none of them alone can solve the educational problem.

What constitutes good teaching is highly context-dependent. It depends on the subject being taught; the level and depth at which it is taught; the learning goals of the lesson; the age of the students; the size of the classroom; the resources available; the personality, temperament, and skills of the teacher; and even the time of day and the season of the year. All these factors can influence which teaching method is most suitable in order to achieve optimum learning by students.

But just listing the many factors that have an influence on teaching already gives us a clue as to what makes for a good teacher. A good teacher must necessarily be aware of the need to develop a range of expertise in the various teaching methods available and an awareness of how to select the most appropriate ones for a particular teaching situation. There are many metaphors that can be invoked to capture the essence of the various teaching methods.[10]

TEACHING METAPHORS

The most familiar metaphor is that of the *sage* dispensing authoritative knowledge and wisdom. In this model, the teacher is the authority on whatever the subject being taught. The job of the student is to listen and absorb the knowledge, asking the occasional question. Good teaching consists of the teacher's presenting expert knowledge of the subject matter clearly and in an organized manner. This requires the skills of logic, organization, and public speaking.

This model is the dominant one in colleges, with its primarily lecture-driven format, although high school teachers frequently adopt it as well. The good teacher is thus defined as the one who gives good lectures. It is up to the students to make good use of the knowledge they hear from the teacher. The teacher demonstrates his or her understanding of the subject to the student, and the student learns by emulating the teacher. The quality of the classroom can be evaluated by observing largely what the teacher alone does, and as long as the students are well behaved and listening, what they do is marginal to the learning process. In this model, teaching is a performance, and the teacher is a performer, not unlike an actor or musician.

Another class of teaching metaphors consists of the teacher as *manager*, *coach*, or *orchestra conductor* (or *maestro*). These metaphors conjure up the vision of the teacher as someone who leads and inspires others to achieve. Here the teacher does not necessarily demonstrate how it is done and indeed may not even be an expert in the area being studied, although that undoubtedly helps. The teacher sets the goals for students and uses a judicious mix of coaxing, cajoling, rewards, threats, and punishment to get them to achieve at high levels. This role requires a different kind of personality and skills than the sage model. While the sage can be aloof from the students and still be considered successful, the coach requires a very people-oriented personality.

Portrayals of good teachers in popular films (*Dead Poets Society*, *Stand and Deliver*, *Mr. Holland's Opus*) and television tend to favor the coach or maestro model of teacher because it makes for heartwarming drama, since the teacher, by the sheer force of his or her personality, can produce a transformative effect on even the most passive, resistant, or inexpert of students.

The third class of teacher metaphor is that of a *midwife* or *guide*. In this role, the prime responsibility for learning falls on the student. It is the student who has to set the goals and initiate the learning process, while the teacher is there to provide assistance when needed. It is the responsibility of the student to deliver the baby (so to speak) or make the journey. The teacher can provide encouragement, support, and guidance at crucial points but cannot, and does not, take on the learning responsibility herself.

To my mind, it is a fourth metaphor that captures the most important, but often overlooked, aspect of learning. It is that of the teacher as *gardener*, with the plant symbolizing the learning of the student. I like this metaphor because I believe learning is an inherently voluntary act, and you can no more force students to learn than you can force a plant to grow or force someone to love you. If that were not true, one might expect that the best learning would occur in prison schools since the "students" there can be coerced to do almost anything.

All a gardener can do is create those conditions in which plants flourish. A good gardener understands the nature and needs of the plant. He knows how to prepare the soil, when to plant, when to water, and when to prune. He recognizes when the plant is not flourishing and knows what to do to rejuvenate it. But he also realizes that no amount of persuasion has any influence on the plant's growth. There has to be a material change in the environment of the plant in order to change the condition of the plant.

A good teacher should mostly have the skills of a good gardener, although there are occasions when the skills involved with the other metaphors also need to be called upon. In order to become good gardeners, we need to look at the research that explores what makes for successful learning environments, because the primary task for the teacher is to create the conditions that make students *want* to learn. Many of the more popular suggestions for improving learning, however, are based not on the gardening metaphor, but on the coaching metaphor, and it is important to appreciate the different practices that arise from their adoption.

With the coaching model, what is popularly known as "tough love" is the ideal to be aimed for. Teachers tend to want to believe that, in order to get students to learn, they need to be tough about enforcing rules for classroom behavior and work, and fair in the implementation of the rules. If my own conversations with teachers are representative, this feeling seems to be held more strongly among teachers of lower-achieving students in urban districts, who see themselves as having to establish discipline and control before they can even think about teaching.

But power in the classroom is a tricky issue, and it is not clear that trying to establish discipline in the traditional sense (where students "behave" because of the fear of consequences) is the best option. Virginia Richmond and James McCroskey emphasize that students have more power than we realize and that the more we try to exercise direct authority and control, the more likely it is that they will devise other ways to thwart us. The teacher who prides herself on maintaining discipline in her classroom may be inadvertently contributing to disruptions elsewhere in the school or community. At the very least, students can rebel by deliberately not learning or by generating moderate levels of classroom incivilities that do not rise to punishable levels of defiance but spoil the classroom environment nonetheless.[11]

As has been stated many times previously, learning is an inherently voluntary act, and any teacher who does not realize this and take it into account in teaching practice is doomed to failure. Certainly we can force some (or even most) students to do specific things (such as turning up for class, sitting quietly, doing assignments) by threatening them with punishments if they fail. Or we can bribe some students to do these same things by promising them good grades, elite colleges, and future wealth. But threats and bribes do not work for all students. What is worse, even if such practices do result in students' "working" as prescribed, real learning may not be taking place at all, however good test scores may be.

What such coercive practices frequently lead to is what is sometimes derided as "bulimic learning": students assimilate information just long enough to be regurgitated on tests, and then promptly forget it. What goes on in many classrooms is this form of faux learning, with teachers and students alike going through the motions of what they imagine learning to be, rather than the real thing.

The current emphasis on accountability in schools, with its concomitant emphasis on standardized proficiency testing, is really an expanded version of this tough-love philosophy applied to entire states. It is hoped that the threat of not being promoted to higher grades or not graduating from high school will be sufficient to motivate students to learn, and that the threat of losing students, having schools shut down, losing their jobs, or other similar sanctions will be sufficient to make teachers and administrators do a better job of teaching.

I believe that not only will these methods fail to achieve their goal, but they will also, in the long run, result in lower levels of learning. Threats and rewards may have some short-term value in making students and teachers increase their level of activity and follow rules. But if students do not want to learn and if teachers do not know how to spark interest in learning, then all this frenetic activity will be for nothing. What is worse, these tactics will also dampen whatever little interest there is in learning.

Recall from the previous chapter that black students already know what they need to do to succeed in school. For a variety of reasons, they don't do these things despite the promised rewards and despite the threats that accompany failure. What makes us think that applying more, or even different kinds of, threats is likely to succeed?

IMPORTANCE OF LEARNING FOR ITS OWN SAKE

To my mind, the only long-term solution to the problem of student underachievement lies in making students want to learn, not because of what they might get if they succeed on tests or because of fear of what might happen if they fail, but because they find learning interesting for its own sake. The act of learning has to win (in terms of emotional and intellectual satisfaction) in comparison to the other things that compete for student attention.

This may strike many as an unrealistic expectation, if not as hopelessly idealistic. Skeptics will ask if we can really expect learning to be chosen over, say, watching television or hanging out at the mall, but why do we have such low expectations for our students? All of us in the field of education are believers in, and practitioners of, lifelong learning. We know that learning is enjoyable for its own sake, and we often choose to do it at the expense of other, more superficially entertaining activities. We know that reading for learning and reading for pleasure need not be mutually exclusive. Why do we assume that the overwhelming majority of students are not like us in this regard?

The fact that our current experience tends to make us think that students do not enjoy learning is really an indication of how poorly we have been teaching students, not an indication of how disinterested in learning students are. If we are to make any serious dent in the problems of education, we have to learn how to make learning interesting for everyone, not just for the few (like us) who happened to stumble onto this secret.

I believe that the primary skill a teacher must have is the ability to instill in students a desire to learn for its own sake. But to find out how to do this, we need to find out what learning is. So a more promising approach to solving the seemingly intractable achievement-gap problem might be to start with the more fundamental question of what learning involves and what conditions are conducive to learning, and then, based on a deeper understanding of this subtle process, see what promising educational strategies emerge.

LEARNING AND THE BRAIN

We ought to pay attention to what research on the brain suggests for how people learn.[12] What is going on in the mind of the learner when she or he is learning new things? Learning involves changing the very physical structure of our brains, and we need to be aware of the studies that illuminate how our brain incorporates new information, transforms and integrates it with our prior knowledge, and creates the resulting synthesis that we call "knowledge." "[T]he quality of information to which one is exposed and the amount of information one acquires is reflected throughout one's life in the structure of the brain."[13] In other words, the brain contains a record of what we have learned.

The research that is coming out on these topics is significant. The recent book by my colleague James Zull, called *The Art of Changing the Brain*, recognizes up front that learning involves changing the actual physical structure of the brain, and it shows how teachers would benefit from knowing how the brain stores and retrieves knowledge.[14] The implications of brain research for education can easily be overblown, so I should state right at the outset that studying the way the brain creates and stores knowledge is nowhere close to providing us with a blueprint for how we should teach, and it is unlikely that it ever will. But that does not mean it does not provide some general guidance.

At the risk of oversimplifying, we can say that the brain constructs knowledge by forming links (called synapses) that connect brain cells (neurons). These networks of neurons connected by synapses come into being by two methods. The first stage occurs in the early periods of development in childhood and consists of rapid overproduction of synapses followed by selective loss. This *pruning* of synapses is done when human experience selects those synapses worth retaining and allows those not required to atrophy. The neural networks that remain constitute the sensory and cognitive base for later learning. An analogy to this process might be that of a sculpture in which a block of marble is turned into a statue by removing those pieces of marble that are unnecessary. In this case, human experience is the "sculptor" that determines which pieces of marble should be retained.

It appears that certain types of learning have time windows during which they can occur more easily, which explains, for example, why accents are acquired and lost easily in childhood but are hard to change as adults. Clearly the nature of the environment experienced during this early stage has a strong influence on the structure of the brain, and varied and stimulating environments are more beneficial for early brain development than are more sterile, barren ones.[15]

The second way in which networks change is by the *addition* of new synapses that connect already existing networks. This is especially important in later life. This aspect is driven by experience, and the learning process plays a crucial role here in making these connections and forming synapses. New experiences result in new synapses starting to form and branching out. Since the strength of the synapses increases with repeated firing of the neurons, creating repeated opportunities for practice is likely to result in more lasting learning. That repetition is important in teaching will not come as a surprise to anyone. But this does not imply that we should just drill students with repetitive exercises of the same thing. While that might increase the strength of a single synapse (or a few synapses), that comes at too large a cost, since such a process will create boredom in the student's mind. Simple repetition will not provide the different branching of synapses that lead to greater chances of students' seeing and appreciating connections. Students need to be emotionally engaged with the material being learned so that they want to try out their ideas and test them in different ways.

Since the nature of environments strongly influences the amount of learning, an increased variety of the situations experienced by students will tend to broaden the scale of the networks in addition to strengthening them. What should be done to achieve this is to focus on a few key ideas and repeat those ideas in new and enriched contexts. This enables students to discover new connections among formerly disconnected ideas while strengthening the basic ideas the teacher is trying to convey.

So learning actually reorganizes the structure of the brain. What is interesting is that currently popular models of learning and teaching that are bundled under the label "constructivist education" (which is based on the idea that each student constructs his or her own knowledge based on how he or she interprets his or her experiences) conform closely to the model by which brains grow.

CREATING EXPERT LEARNERS

In order to develop appropriate teaching strategies, we also have to decide what *kind* of learning we value. In the past, it might have been possible to contemplate learning as consisting of acquiring a fairly well-defined body of knowledge. For example, in the era when the Great Books curricula were popular, one could point to a set of classic works that remained unchanged and that, if mastered, were believed to provide the foundations of knowledge.

I am not sure if such a simple view was ever really true of education, but it is clearly untenable now. The explosive growth of knowledge and the shifting of emphasis to the sciences and social sciences mean that there is no longer a canon of books, no fixed set of eternal verities that one can seek to acquire in a finite span of time.

In this era, we need to replace the goals of education from creating "traditional experts," defined as people who have mastery of a body of knowledge and who know the answers to important questions in that field, to creating *"expert learners"* (or "accomplished novices"). Expert learners are people who are able to approach new situations flexibly, are able to learn throughout their lifetimes, and are skilled at acquiring new knowledge quickly and efficiently. It is the lack of such skills that causes some students to fall behind and results in achievement gaps. Remedial instruction, with its traditional emphasis on acquiring factual knowledge using lower-level learning skills, can actually inhibit the development of expert learning skills. While knowing a specific body of factual knowledge is often important, we need to pay close attention to *how* that knowledge is acquired as well, since that has a strong influence on subsequent learning.

Expert learners demonstrate the following characteristics.[16] They have an awareness of the difference between understanding and memorizing material, and they know which mental strategies to use in each case. They have the ability to recognize which parts of a text are difficult, which in turn dictates where to start reading and how much time to spend on different parts. They have an awareness of the need to take problems and examples from the text, order them randomly, and then try to solve them. They know when they don't understand so that help can be sought from an expert. They know when the expert's explanations solve the immediate learning problems. In short, expert learners interact with the material, creating a dialogue, posing questions, and seeking answers.

Less-skilled (or novice) learners, by contrast, do not always appreciate the difference between memorization and comprehension and are unaware that different strategies are required for each case, they are less likely to notice whether texts were easy or difficult, and they are less likely to use self-tests and self-questioning as sources of feedback to correct misconceptions.

People who have studied expert learners observe that they also share certain other characteristics, such as focusing on identifying meaningful features and patterns rather than specific facts.[17] For example, when a chessboard arrangement from the middle of an actual game was presented for view for a limited period of time and then removed from sight, chess experts could reproduce the position on the board with remarkable accuracy when compared with novices. That this was not due to a more prodigious memory for the "facts" of the situation (i.e., the number and types of pieces on the board and their locations) became clear when the experiment was repeated with pieces placed at random and not from an actual game. The experts were then no better than the novices at reproducing the board arrangement. The experts, unlike the novices, made sense of the pieces and their positions in the context of a deeper understanding of the strategy of the game. The "facts" were then *reconstructed* (not simply recalled) in accordance with their model.

In the case of physics, when presented with problems to solve, experts tend to initially try and identify the underlying principles applicable to the problem, while novices tend to focus on the superficial features of the problem. Expert physicists also try to find a single key idea to solving the problem and, stimulated by this idea, recall related concepts and equations in a cascade of connected clusters. Novices, on the other hand, tended to produce equations sequentially, not in relation to one another, and in a trial-and-error manner, rather than as part of a coherent problem-solving strategy.

In the case of mathematics, experts try to *understand* the problem first, while novices immediately try to mechanically apply the algorithmic rules they have learned.

In another example, historians (medievalists, Asian-studies experts, and Americanists) and AP (advanced placement) high school students were given a test of facts about the American revolution. The AP students tended to outscore the medievalists and the Asian-studies experts. But then all were asked to make sense of certain historical documents. "The historians excelled in the elaborateness of understandings they developed in their ability to pose alternative explanations for events and in their use of corroborating evidence."[18] When asked to select which of three pictures best reflected their understanding of the battle of Lexington, historians looked on this as the "quintessential epistemological exercise. . . . They knew that no single document or picture could tell the story of history," so they went back and forth between the documents and the pictures, carefully weighing alternatives and the reasons for them before making a choice. However, the AP students had no systematic way of making sense of contradictory or competing claims or of formulating reasoned interpretations of historical documents. They instead approached the problem in a manner similar to finding the answer on a multiple-choice test.[19]

Expert learners tend to have the ability to fluently retrieve *relevant* knowledge, while novices lack the knowledge of when to apply the knowledge they have. Experts also have conditional knowledge that cannot be reduced to a set of facts and propositions. Ask an expert in any field to list all the things they do when faced with a new situation or problem, and they will find it hard to make such a list because so much of their thinking is based on acquired intuition based on a vast array of experiences. Or if they do make a list, they will not realize that they are leaving out a whole set of implicit steps.

A professor of nursing told me how she was asked to make a training video for dealing with newborn babies and their mothers, and in preparing for this she was asked to make a list of the specific steps she goes through in interviewing them. She prepared this list as best as she could, but when she actually did the examination for the camera, she realized that in just making small talk with the mother before the formal examination began that she had already gained important information that guided her subsequent investigation. She had not been aware of how much implicit knowledge she routinely acquired by absorbing subtle cues, and she did not realize what an important (but unrecognized) role this knowledge played in her decision making during the examination.

Expert learners also practice *metacognition*, which is the ability to monitor one's own understanding and know when it is not adequate. For example, a Lincoln scholar, another historian, and high school history teachers were asked to read and interpret a set of documents about Abraham Lincoln and his view of slavery. The Lincoln scholar recognized that "this [was] a complex issue that, for Lincoln, involved conflicts between enacted law (the constitution), natural law (encoded in the Declaration of Independence), and divine law (assumptions about basic rights)." Using this conceptual framework enabled the scholar to make sense of the documents.

The non-Lincoln historian and teachers, on the other hand, initially tried to harmonize discrepant events by invoking contemporary ideas (speech writers, press conferences, and spin doctors). But the historian eventually realized that these conceptual categories were inadequate and went beyond these initial analyses, adopting the working hypothesis that the discrepancies might be due less to Lincoln's duplicity and more to the historian's own ignorance of the nineteenth century. After a lot of work, he managed to arrive at the more sophisticated position of the Lincoln scholar. The history teachers, unlike the scholars, did not have the level of metacognitive or expert-learning skills to get beyond simplistic analyses and arrive at a deeper understanding.[20]

Helping students who fall behind acquire expert learning skills is, in the long run, far more important than making sure they learn specific facts. The goal of creating such adaptive experts requires us to *simultaneously* teach knowledge as well as the ability to transfer expertise to new situations. Students need to learn abstract principles in addition to specific facts, and striking an appropriate balance between the two is important. While facts might be important in a particular learning situation, we also want students, while learning those facts, to simultaneously acquire learning skills that can be transferred to other learning situations. Learning that is overcontextualized can inhibit such transfer, while abstract interpretations of knowledge help promote transfer.

For example, in teaching mathematics, teachers often resort to having students do worksheets with lots of problems, essentially repeating the same idea. In one of my classroom visits to a Cleveland high school, the lesson dealt with how to convert between a decimal representation of a number and a percentage representation of the same number. Almost the entire class consisted of the students doing worksheets that were essentially repetitions of the same problem. They were given the decimal form of a number and asked to find the percentage form (by multiplying the original number by 100), and then they were given the percentage form of a number and asked to find the decimal form (by dividing by 100).

What would the students learn from this time-consuming exercise? They would get better at multiplying and dividing by 100. They *may* know what to do if, sometime in the future, they are confronted by one form of a number and asked to convert it to the other, though it is likely they would have to guess whether they should multiply or divide, and by which number. But the most important lesson they would learn is that mathematics is mind-numbingly boring.

The reason for doing this exercise was not given to the students, nor was the exercise embedded in any real-life situation that might have given it relevance. There was no attempt to give the students a sense of what a decimal number or a percent *represents*, what it *means*. Presumably the idea behind the lesson was that by repeating the exercise over and over again, the ability to convert from decimals to percentages and vice versa would become automatic. But acquiring a sense of meaning is essential if students are to retain what they learn and have more than rote knowledge.

The importance of acquiring meaning is illustrated by a story from my own experience. I was teaching a physics laboratory class, and a group of students came to me to check their results. They had been required to collect a set of seven or eight measurements and compute the average value. I briefly glanced at the numbers and said that they had made an error in their calculations. The students laboriously repeated the calculation in front of me and discovered that they had, indeed, made an error, and they were quite impressed that I had been able to determine it instantaneously and seemingly by magic. The (not nearly so impressive) reason that I was able to do so was because the erroneous "average" they had originally calculated was larger than the largest number that had gone into computing the average. That this cannot be so is obvious to anyone who understands the *meaning* of the concept of average. But not having that meaning, the students could only mechanically carry out the steps of the operation, not understanding what they were doing or why.

Too many facts or too much problem solving following a fixed set of procedures can actually be bad for deep learning. When given a new situation, those who have had some abstract instruction do better than those who have not.[21] Lion Gardiner discusses how students in college-engineering-degree programs typically are assigned about 3,000 problems to work on during their course of study. Their instructors presumably think that by working so many problems the students will abstract the general principles underlying problem solving and be able to apply these principles to novel problems. In actual practice, though, what happens is that students essentially learn 3,000 problem-solving schemas, not the underlying principles, and are thus not able to transfer the knowledge effectively.[22]

Learning also cannot be rushed. The complex cognitive activity of information integration requires time. More time spent on a topic usually correlates with more learning. An important reason that students in honors algebra classes learn more than students in regular algebra classes is that students typically spend more time in the former (65 hours for regular algebra versus 250 hours for honors).[23] But what the Trends in International Mathematics and Science Study (TIMSS) revealed is that rushing through content is exactly what occurs in U.S. classrooms. The K–12 curriculum is characterized as a mile wide and an inch thick, and student textbooks are ever-growing monsters, with the result being that teachers speed through many topics without giving students time to achieve mastery of any. Then, the following year, the next teacher has to do "remedial" work to make up for what the students were supposed to have learned the previous year but did not. This results in even less time for the new teacher to cover what he or she is supposed to cover, which results in even more rushing, and so on.

Attempts to cover too many topics too quickly may hinder learning and subsequent transfer because students (a) learn only isolated facts that are not organized or connected and (b) are introduced to organizing principles that they cannot grasp because they lack enough specific knowledge to make them meaningful. It is a truly vicious cycle.

THE IMPORTANCE OF PRIOR KNOWLEDGE

Perhaps the prime reason for poor teaching is that we fail to understand students. This failure comes in many ways. One is that we deal with students as we wish them to be as opposed to how they really are. We treat them as if they were blank slates because working on that assumption makes our life easier. Under this assumption, all that students need to do is to sit quietly and listen carefully to us, and they will learn, a convenient model for those who prize order and discipline in the classroom. This ignores the increasingly recognized fact that students at whatever age have developed highly complex knowledge schemas before they step foot into any classroom. All learning and teaching has to take this into account.

For example, there is a well-known and revealing video called *A Private Universe* (produced by the Harvard-Smithsonian Center for Astrophysics) which interviews graduates and faculty during the commencement ceremonies at Harvard University, asking them questions about why we have different seasons during the year. The respondents (all of whom are the successful products of elite school systems for at least part of their school careers) provide answers centered around one basic misconception: that in summer Earth is closer to the Sun (and thus days are warmer) and in winter it is farther from the Sun (and thus colder). It is highly unlikely that they have been explicitly taught this wrong information. In fact, science textbooks, science standards, and science teaching explain clearly the correct reasons as to why we have seasons. But the misconceptions survive and outlive all the direct and explicit teaching to the contrary that students receive.

Students, whatever their age, come into the classroom with complex knowledge structures of which even they are frequently unaware. Many teachers are not prepared to deal with students' prior knowledge. Teachers either ignore this prior knowledge or think that by simply asserting that the prior knowledge is wrong they have effectively neutralized it. But dealing with prior knowledge is not that easy. It is one of the most important things instructors have to deal with. The prior knowledge of students, if appreciated and understood and taken into account in developing teaching strategies, can be one of the greatest assets in learning. But if the teacher ignores it, then it can become one of the greatest hindrances.

One way that prior knowledge can inhibit learning is because the way knowledge was acquired in one area may not be applicable in another and thus can prevent transfer. For example, children initially learn numbers in the form of integers and learn to sequence them using counting principles. They then move on to fractions. But the principles used in dealing with fractions are not consistent with the counting methods previously encountered with integers.[24] One cannot, for example, use counting-based algorithms in sequencing fractions. Doing so results in students' getting hopelessly confused. The introduction to fractions may be the first major hurdle that causes students to disengage from mathematics and to think that it is not for them.

But one cannot blame students who try to apply counting-based sequencing processes (which worked so well for them with integers) when they confront fractions. It is natural for students in learning anything new to apply strategies that have worked before, just like generals who devise military strategies based on their experience with previous wars. Simply asserting that counting-based strategies no longer apply and should not be used for fractions also has limited effectiveness. A good teacher is one who recognizes the importance of these issues and devises teaching strategies that enable students to realize for themselves the need to develop new methods and algorithms to deal with new situations.

Effective teachers know how to tap into students existing knowledge in order to make new information meaningful.[25] In the absence of this skill, teachers tend to depend on textbook publishers for curriculum decisions, such as the scope and sequencing of topics. Experienced teachers also know how to make the most of learning situations, those "teachable moments" that arise spontaneously in all classrooms as part of the daily routine.

An interesting but little-known experiment is that of Louis Benezet, the superintendent of a small school district in New Hampshire, who was appalled at the inability of middle school students to solve simple mathematics problems. He was particularly struck by seeing students instinctively resort to applying the algorithms they had been taught, even in situations where the algorithm was either inapplicable or when a little thought would have given them the answer without the need for any mathematics formalism.

In his experiment, Benezet decided to dispense with formal mathematics instruction altogether in grades K–5 for some schools. (This was back in 1929, when superintendents had more flexibility in what they could do.) Instead he allowed children to play various games or deal with money transactions in which the mathematics concepts that had previously been taught formally occurred naturally as part of the activities involved. For example, the "average value" of a quantity frequently appears as part of sports statistics and requires understanding division and fractions in order to calculate and use them. Because students wanted and needed to learn these mathematics strategies in order to play the games well, they quickly learned what was necessary.

Formal mathematics algorithms were only introduced in grade 6. What Benezet found was that because students already had an intuitive idea of the meaning of the mathematics operations involved, in just one year they learned material normally covered in six years of formal instruction. In addition, the students had a better understanding of mathematics because they saw the relationship between the formal operations and their intuitive understanding.[26]

WHAT MAKES FOR GOOD TEACHING

Real learning is driven by a *desire to know*, and a teacher who does not have the knowledge or skills to spark such desires in students is hopelessly disadvantaged. The book *How People Learn* provides guidelines on what is necessary to become a really effective teacher. In this summary of the research literature, a group of academics analyzed the research evidence from areas of cognitive science, education, and brain research and found a suggestive convergence of ideas from the three fields. The research evidence is quite clear that three components go into making effective teachers: *content knowledge*, *generic teaching skills*, and *pedagogical content knowledge*.

It is easy to understand the benefits of a teacher having good content knowledge. It is extremely hard to teach with flexibility and resourcefulness if teachers themselves have difficulty understanding the content they are teaching. Teachers do not have to be content experts, but they do need to have a sufficient level of comfort with the material. I have conducted enough professional-development courses to realize that, at least in the mathematics and science areas, many teachers are unprepared in their assigned subjects, some woefully so. Such teachers tend to take refuge in a textbook- and lecture-dominated teaching mode because this kind of teaching maintains teacher control of the flow of information and lessens the chance that students will get engaged, explore new ideas, and ask questions, thus exposing the teacher's own ignorance. Little learning occurs in such passive classrooms.

It is an interesting statistic that teachers with higher test scores of their own are more effective than teachers with lower test scores.[27] It is not clear why this is so. Perhaps it is related to the importance of content knowledge, or maybe it is related to the sense of self-efficacy of the teacher. Teachers who are confident of their own abilities (and test scores are often used as measures of competency) may be more willing to try more innovative teaching methods, while teachers who are insecure with their own content knowledge may be more likely to take refuge in the textbook.

The second necessary component to successful teaching is the acquisition of certain generic teaching skills that are conducive to what is known as "active learning" by students: well-structured cooperative learning classrooms, knowledge of how to implement hands-on and inquiry-based instruction, knowing what it takes to create conditions for enhancing intrinsic as opposed to extrinsic motivation in students,[28] and the ability to prepare curricula that enable students to feel challenged and to also provide appropriate levels of guidance and support to enable them to succeed.

There are also some very specific skills that teachers can develop. They should learn how to increase wait times so as to enable students to reflect more thoughtfully on questions. Most teachers wait only for a second or so after asking a question before either answering the question themselves or calling upon the same handful of students who are eager to respond. Minority students in integrated classrooms participate more when the wait time is longer. This improves their performance and, even more importantly, also changes teacher perceptions of them.[29] Teachers should also learn the value of providing corrective, *neutral* feedback to their students, which is even more valuable than wait times. Teachers who practice this are less able to predict students' later achievements, and this had positive effects on performance, especially for minority students.[30]

The final component, and the one that is frequently overlooked, is the need for the teacher to have pedagogical content knowledge in the specific subjects being taught. In any subject or topic, students arrive with preconceived knowledge that may conflict with what the instructor is trying to teach (the prior knowledge issue we spoke about in the previous section). This knowledge is often so deeply buried in the student's mind that he or she may not even be aware of it, but these discipline-specific learning obstacles strongly influence what is learned and, if not taken into account, can nullify teachers' best efforts.

For example, in teaching the subject of electricity, a teacher should be aware that most people believe implicitly and strongly that a battery provides the same amount of current in all situations. They also believe that electric current comes out of a socket and is used up by the appliance. I was incredulous when I first heard of these beliefs because no science textbook teaches such things, and it was inconceivable to me how anyone could acquire such erroneous ideas. But many years of teaching electricity to teachers have convinced me that such beliefs are widespread. Now that I have acquired a greater appreciation of how people learn, these beliefs do not seem nearly so preposterous to me as they did a decade ago. After all, in the course of their everyday lives, people try to make sense of phenomena and build (often unconsciously) mental models that satisfy them. The idea that a battery produces a fixed amount of current, which is then used up, does have an empirical basis and makes sense to people. If a teacher tries to teach electricity without having his or her students examine the consequences of this hidden and erroneous belief, much of that teaching will be wasted.

In my own experience with teaching electricity to teachers (and which is supported by extensive research by others[31]), I have found it necessary to provide them with experimental situations in which their prior beliefs fail as explanations for the phenomena they observe, thus forcing them to develop new models to represent their revised understanding. And it cannot be done just once. It has to be done *repeatedly* in a variety of contexts before the new models replace their prior convictions.

The same is true for any subject, however esoteric. No student is ever a blank slate. They all come with preconceptions, and a teacher needs to learn what the specific preconceptions are for that particular topic and, instead of ignoring them, know how to use these preconceptions to more effectively teach students.

PRINCIPLES OF GOOD TEACHING

Arthur Chickering and Steve Ehrmann have studied the literature on what makes for good college teaching and have summarized them under *The Seven Principles of Good Teaching*. These are as follows: encourage contact between students and faculty, develop reciprocity and cooperation among students, encourage active learning, give prompt feedback, emphasize time on task, communicate high expectations, and respect diverse talents and ways of learning.[32]

Notable in this list is the *absence* of features that are commonly viewed as necessary components of good teaching: coercion and authoritarianism; an emphasis on rewards and threats; and theatricality, showmanship, and dramatic skill. Instead, the focus is on how to create the conditions that make students want to learn for its own sake. All the principles emphasize the importance of creating a positive classroom atmosphere by minimizing direct instruction and increasing cooperative learning and using more hands-on, inquiry-based curricula and instructional materials.

These methods also emphasize the importance of giving students time to learn and emphasize the importance of having students achieve mastery over the subject matter as opposed to superficial familiarity. These features also emphasize *deep learning* as opposed to *surface learning*, important distinctions that were elucidated by the research of Marton and Säljö back in 1976.[33]

Educator John Biggs summarizes the characteristics of these two contrasting modes and the conditions that give rise to these two kinds of learning. In the surface-learning mode, students learn in anticipation of outcomes, concentrating anxiously on the facts and details that might be asked. Thus they "skate along the surface of the text." They try to get assignments out of the way with minimal trouble while appearing to meet requirements. The result of this kind of learning is that students remember a set of disjointed facts and do not understand the point the author was making. Conditions that result in this kind of learning are as follows: insufficient time and/or too high a workload, misunderstanding requirements (e.g., thinking that factual recall is adequate), high anxiety, a genuine inability to understand particular content at a high level, subject taught in a piecemeal fashion and not focusing on structure, assessments that are used mainly to measure independent facts, teaching and assessing in a way that encourages cynicism, and creating undue anxiety or low expectations of success.

In the deep-learning mode, however, students set out to understand the meaning of what the author is trying to say. Thus they go below the surface of the text. The results of this kind of learning are that students see the big picture and also see how the facts and details make the author's case. The conditions that are conducive to this kind of learning occur when it is made clear to students what the objectives are and where they are going, when students feel free to focus on the task and are not pressured by urgent and ill-conceived assessments, and when students can work collaboratively and in dialogue with others.[34]

Biggs points out that some students come into our classes already convinced of the value of the deep-learning mode and committed to using it (he calls them "academic students"), but most students may not be like that. He says that "good teaching is getting most students to use the higher-level cognitive processes that the more academic students use spontaneously."[35]

ASSESSMENTS

Assessments also play an important role. The trap with assessments is that we tend to focus our attention on what can be assessed easily rather than measuring things that are worth knowing. Multiple-choice testing of low-level information is popular because it is easy to do, we are familiar with it, and the assessments have a spurious air of objectivity. But these kinds of assessments are suitable mainly for knowledge of factual information. Many of the things we really value in student learning cannot be easily measured using such multiple-choice tests.

A list of other desirable qualities that are worth knowing might include enhanced problem-solving skills, higher-level critical-thinking abilities, the ability to use written language well and thoughtfully, the ability to think through a problem and experiment with solutions, the ability to formulate and articulate ideas verbally in a group setting, knowing how to listen carefully to the ideas of others and respond respectfully to them even if one disagrees, the ability to function well (and help others function well) in groups, the ability to learn something new by yourself, the ability to make formal presentations, and an increased appreciation of values and ethics.

Knowing how well our students can do these things requires a much wider variety of assessment tools than are traditionally used. They also take more time and care to create, and necessarily need to be much more individualized. Creating such assessments takes teachers into territory that is unfamiliar, asking them to do things they were not exposed to when they themselves were students. This can make them quite uncomfortable. They are unlikely to experiment with these different kinds of assessments unless they have guidance and support and are encouraged to experiment.

Most of our current assessments are also *summative*. We assess how well students have learned the previous course material at some instant of time and then move on to the next body of material. *Formative* assessments that give the student useful information on what they know and don't know, benchmarks for recognizing levels of mastery, strategies for achieving mastery, and opportunities for revisiting older material using these new strategies are equally important but rarely used.

Assessments are a necessary part of teaching. Teachers and students alike need to know how far and how well students are progressing toward learning goals. In order to achieve those aims, assessment must be meaningful and provide feedback to students on what needs to improve and how it can be done, and it should also cover the broad spectrum of content and thought processes, not simply those that are easily measured.

But we often forget that providing meaningful feedback to individual students is the main purpose of assessments. Instead, assessments are being used for a whole variety of other purposes that they are not really suitable for. One of the most pernicious uses of student assessment is to rank school districts, buildings, and even teachers. One can immediately see where this will lead. If teachers are ranked on the basis of how well their students perform on standardized tests, teachers will seek to teach those students who already have a good chance of doing well on these standardized such tests. So instead of the most skilled and experienced teachers being asked to teach the students who have fallen the farthest behind, which is the most sensible strategy, such teachers will gravitate to students who are most likely to succeed on their own, such as those from affluent families in the suburbs.

Another negative consequence of using assessments to rank teachers, schools, and districts is that the focus shifts to teaching only those things that will be measured on the tests, a practice scornfully referred to as "teaching to the test." In my view, teaching to the test is not necessarily a bad thing. The important questions that should be asked concern the nature of the test that is being used. If the test is a meaningful measure of important learning goals, then by all means we should teach to it. But most high-stakes tests are inadequate because they necessarily emphasize knowledge that can be assessed using multiple-choice questions, and it has already been argued that such tests measure only a very narrow slice of the full spectrum of learning goals.

ALIGNMENT

Another factor that is often overlooked is the importance of alignment between goals, teaching methods, and assessment. All too often teachers and curriculum directors have high-level goals for students (critical thinking, good writing and speaking skills, good citizenship, etc.) but then teach in a manner that does not give students opportunities to advance toward these goals. Teachers also give assessments that do not measure these desirable qualities. Rather than outright bad teaching, it is this lack of alignment between teaching goals, teaching strategies, and assessments that has been suggested by some scholars as the main cause of poor student achievement.[36]

For example, how are students expected to become more critical thinkers if they spend most of their time sitting passively listening to their teachers? How can they develop good writing and speaking skills if they are not given repeated opportunities to practice both skills and get knowledgeable feedback on where they need to improve and guidelines for how to improve? How can they learn to respect the rights of others if they are in authoritarian classrooms in which all decisions are made by teachers and administrators? How can they learn ethics if they never get to make decisions that affect others? How can they become good citizens if they work alone in their classrooms, where interaction with other students is discouraged, or are placed in active competition with their peers for limited rewards (either grades or other favors)?

When teachers come to me with concerns about not being effective in their teaching, I ask them the following question: Can you name the key ideas that you want your students to learn from your course? I insist that the number of ideas should not be more than five. It is interesting that most teachers find this hard to do (at least initially) because they do not think this way in planning their teaching. Instead they tend to focus on creating a list of topics to be covered, and such an approach inevitably tends to create an ever-growing list as the knowledge base of each subject expands.

Once they have created their list of (at most) five key ideas (or organizing principles), I then ask them to list all the different topics and experiences they can think of that shed light and perspective on these key ideas and then to structure the entire course on how to use these topics and activities, in progressively complex ways, to illustrate the key ideas. I also ask them to construct assessments that focus on measuring student progress toward understanding these key ideas and to use the assessments not merely as measures of where students are, but also as opportunities to give students detailed feedback on what they seem to know, what they need to work on, and what resources they should access in order to get closer to the learning goals.

I also suggest that the way they teach should reflect these broader goals. If, for example, they want to develop critical-thinking skills, it is of not much benefit to use the lecture format as the main form of instruction. Critical thinking is developed when people get the opportunity to try out their ideas and have them tested in the crucible of discussion, with give and take from others. This will occur in a positive manner only if cooperative-learning skills have been developed and the classroom is one in which risk taking and student involvement is encouraged.

I want to emphasize that I do not think the lecture method of teaching is bad in itself. There are no good or bad teaching methods, just appropriate or inappropriate ones. A good lecture can be a wonderful thing. Like all teaching methods, it has advantages in specific situations. It can communicate a large amount of material efficiently; it can be used to supplement or elaborate the curriculum; it is good if the material has to be organized or presented in a particular way; it can provide an introduction to unfamiliar areas; it is very efficient for expert-to-expert transmission; it can be used to present new material or material not available elsewhere or that is hard to discover because of originality, complexity, or difficulty; and it can be used to arouse interest in the subject.[37] Students who have already grappled with specific information relevant to a topic, for example, can learn a lot from an organizing lecture.[38]

But lectures, like all teaching methods, have their downsides. Student attention wanders periodically and inevitably decays with time, starting at about 10 minutes into the lecture. Lectures tend to promote lower-level learning of factual information and make the unwarranted assumption that all students need the same information, presented orally at the same pace, impersonally and without dialogue with the presenter. Lectures assume that students have high memory capacity, the same prior knowledge, and good note-taking strategies and skills, and are not susceptible to information-processing overload. Also, entertaining and clear lectures can mislead listeners about the complexity of the material being presented.[39]

The problem is not with the lecture mode itself. It is that the lecture form is used even in teaching situations where it is of little value or is incompatible with the learning goals.

The idea that the best learning occurs when course content, methods of teaching, and assessments should all center on a few key ideas has been around for many years. In some ways, it is so obvious that it should be barely worth stating. What is shocking is that teachers react to these suggestions as if they were revelations. And I cannot really blame them, since I too did not really think of planning my courses and teaching along these lines when I first started teaching. This is a measure of how far we have strayed from the fundamental role of teachers as being to help students develop in an all-around way. We have instead become accustomed to seeing ourselves as purveyors of information, enforcers of discipline, and raters of students.

MOTIVATION

Student motivation to learn is something else that is often not properly addressed in designing learning environments. It is not that the topic of motivation is ignored. On the contrary, when teachers are asked what their biggest teaching challenge is, they usually respond that it is how to deal with unmotivated students. The problem is that student motivation is far too often viewed in two different but erroneous ways. One view of student motivation is that it is something the student is born with or acquires in the home at an early age. It is perceived as something the student brings with him or her into the classroom and lies outside the control of the teacher.

At the other extreme is the view that the teacher can control motivation by external means, using either rewards or punishments. This view is prevalent among those who view teaching via the coach metaphor. In this model, it is possible for the teacher to motivate students by using the correct mix of rewards and threats of punishment.

Alfie Kohn cites evidence against both of these attitudes.[40] He argues against the latter view by showing that it is *intrinsic* motivation (the desire to do something for its own sake) that leads to true learning and that *extrinsic* motivators (i.e., rewards and threats) actually inhibit and stifle learning. It is not hard to understand why this might be so. After all, when we offer a reward to a student or threaten him or her with some punishment in relation to some learning-related issue, what are we implicitly saying? We are tacitly acknowledging that the learning-related task has no intrinsic interest or value and that no one would want to do it without these extrinsic motivators. Kohn and other researchers[41] give numerous examples of cases where the presence of these extrinsic motivators has adverse effects on what students choose to do and how well they do it.

When rewards are offered for anything, students tend to do only enough to merit the reward. The same thing is true with work. People for whom the paycheck is the only reason to work are the same ones who do only what is expected of them and who leave work exactly at the end of the workday. Research shows similar results with even such a basic function as eating. When children "are cajoled into eating a food and even rewarded or praised for eating it, the child often develops an aversion to the food."[42]

It is not hard to understand why the dependence and emphasis on extrinsic motivators leads to decreased performance and increased achievement gaps. After all, if the only reason to work is because of the reward, then the amount of work you do will depend on how much you value the reward. Students who do not place much value on the rewards are unlikely to want to do much work. As shown in the research by Ogbu and others, for a variety of reasons the reward system offered by schools does not have much attraction for black students, so it should not be surprising that they do not do as well in school. But rather than abandoning a failed strategy, what is being advocated is an even more draconian system of rewards and punishments, with more testing and more stringent requirements. Not only will these attempts fail to close the gap, but they may even result in its increase.

Any thoughtful teacher knows that real learning and high levels of achievement cannot be forced; they only occur when the student wants to do them. So the first thing that teachers have to learn to do is wean themselves away from the pervasive practice of giving rewards. We probably will not be able to do away with them completely. After all, we live and work in a milieu that is saturated with grades and other rewards, and suddenly dispensing with them entirely might be resented by the students themselves, since they too have been immersed in that culture all their lives. But there is no question that most teachers have completely internalized the rewards system and have carried it well beyond the minimal requirements necessary. Many classroom teachers have elaborate reward-and-punishment systems that cover almost all aspects of life within, and even outside, the classroom.

What Kohn and others argue is that while student intrinsic motivation cannot be manipulated by extrinsic rewards and threats, it is also not an unchangeable quality that the student either has or does not have when she walks into the classroom. It can be influenced by the learning environment in which students find themselves. So teachers should try and minimize the salience of these unavoidable extrinsic reward mechanisms while focusing their energies on creating the conditions that enhance intrinsic motivation. Kohn argues convincingly that the conditions that allow for intrinsic motivation to flourish can be represented by what he calls "the three Cs": *Content, Choice,* and *Collaboration.*

Content means that we focus on making the subject matter interesting and worth learning for its own sake. As long as students are coerced to come to school and sit in classrooms, teachers can get by without making the subject interesting. But the fact that the classrooms are full by force of law should not absolve us from the responsibility of acting as if attendance was voluntary. All teachers should start planning their classes by asking themselves, "If students were not required to come to my class, how could I teach it so that they would come anyway?" In order to answer that, we have to address other questions such as, Why is this subject matter interesting and important? and How can I teach it in a way that brings out its interesting features and captures the imagination of students? If we cannot answer these questions satisfactorily, then we have to ask ourselves whether we should teach the topic at all, or find ways to learn more about the subject so we can make it interesting. This is not an easy thing to do because we are not accustomed to thinking of teaching this way. But this is the fundamental challenge of teaching. If we do not believe that learning should be a fascinating and rewarding experience for our students, we should not be teaching at all.

This is not to deny that there will always be some material to be learned that is, frankly, dull. But students are not unreasonable. They do not expect everything to be fascinating and are quite willing to learn boring material as long as it is embedded in an interesting problem or is necessary to answer important questions. It is the responsibility of the teacher to find that appropriate and intellectually stimulating context.

The second C, Choice, is another important factor in enhancing intrinsic motivation. We have to support increased student autonomy. It should not be controversial that students, like anybody else, are more likely to put in effort on anything that *they* choose to do rather than what they are told to do. So we should provide students with as much choice as possible in what they learn, how they learn, when they learn, and how they show their learning through the form of assessments. This does not mean that teachers abdicate their responsibilities, which is what many people will initially fear. It does mean that, rather than taking an authoritarian approach to teaching where we feel that we have to decide *everything* for the students, our role should be to provide a broad framework for learning and create flexibility within which the learning goals can be achieved.

Is this unrealistic? Not at all, provided the teacher develops the knowledge and abilities to carry it out successfully. The book *How People Learn* gives examples of how successful teachers do this. It describes the class of a sixth-grade teacher who begins each year by having students answer two questions: What questions do you have about yourself? and What questions do you have about the world? The students then form into small groups where they look for common questions from their individual lists and then rank them in order of interest. Then the whole class gets together and tries to get consensus on what they should investigate that year. The teacher then uses this curriculum map to incorporate the curricular items required of her. For example, one student-generated question (Will I live to be 100 years old?) allowed her to introduce "genetics, family and oral history, actuarial science, statistics and probability, heart disease, cancer, and hypertension. The students had the opportunity to seek out information from family members, friends, experts in various fields, online computer services, and books, as well as the teacher."[43]

In my own teaching, I find that students seize on the opportunity to learn when they are given choices. We also have to realize that our goal should be to enable students to develop the maturity to make these choices responsibly. The only way people learn how to do that is when they actually have opportunities to learn how to make decisions that affect not only them but also those around them. The transition from an authoritarian to a participatory classroom will not be easy. Students and teachers are not used to such a way of operating, and until all become comfortable with it, there will be difficult moments. But think of the payoff when we succeed. We will be creating the kinds of citizens that a truly democratic society needs.

The last C is collaboration. This feature stems from the extensive research that shows collaborative activity as an important constituent of learning. It is natural for people to want to do things together. There is something strange to me about seeing a classroom that is silent, with students seated in rows and discouraged from interacting with one another. Discussing, arguing, trying to forge a consensus, and contributing to problem solving are all important parts of the learning process. To be sure, ultimately learning involves a change in the brain of an individual and as such is an individual process. Some element of individual activity is necessary for learning to occur. But that does not mean students should work in isolation from one another all the time. Interaction with other students is an important element of learning.

Collaboration forms a natural part of learning-cycle models. In the Kolb Learning Cycle[44] there are four stages that the learner repeatedly cycles through: concrete experience, reflective judgment, abstract conceptualization, and active experimentation. What this model suggests is that learning ideally involves going around the cycle. When confronted with a concrete experience (those things we can see, hear, touch, feel, and smell), the brain reacts by drawing upon its store of prior knowledge (memories) that shed some light on the experience (the reflective observation part). The brain then tries to integrate the new experience with its prior knowledge frameworks. It tries to make it "fit" somehow and, in doing so, creates new theories. This is the abstract conceptualization part of the cycle. The brain then tries to test the new theories that have been created, and it does this by active experimentation, using such strategies as "if-then" hypothetico-deductive reasoning to check for consistency and predictive power. If possible, actual experiments might be carried out. The results of such experimentation provide new concrete experiences, and the cycle begins again. It is important to realize that the new cycle is not going over the same ground as the previous one, but is at a more advanced stage. It is perhaps more appropriate to refer to this process as a learning *spiral* rather than *cycle*, since each subsequent cycle is at a more advanced stage of understanding.

The way the learning cycle (or spiral) works is perhaps most easily appreciated in the context of scientific research, where the results of experiments are examined and existing theories and paradigms are modified in order to accommodate the new results, thus leading to new theories. But this is just a specific context for the cycle. The learning-cycle model can be applied to all areas of knowledge, not just science.

While in principle one can go through the cycle on one's own and thus learn in isolation, there is no doubt that interaction with others can be very helpful, especially in the concrete experience and active experimentation stages of the cycle. The merits of cooperative-learning methods have been studied so exhaustively, and its achievements are so robust, that there really is no excuse for any teacher not to structure his or her classroom around it.[45] Student performance improves by about half a standard deviation when cooperative learning methods are used. For example, in a review of the literature, Johnson, Johnson, and Smith show that students who score at the 50th percentile in individualized classrooms score at the 67th percentile in cooperative classrooms.[46]

Cooperative learning is not ignored in schools today. But while it is praised and used often, the nature of its implementation leaves much to be desired. It is either used sporadically or in an ad hoc manner that does not reflect the scholarship behind it. While I do not wish to go into all the theory and practice of cooperative learning, it must be said that it involves a lot more than just putting students together to work in groups. For successful cooperative learning to occur, the teacher must be aware of the conditions that need to be created so that students find the experience rewarding, and the teacher must have the skill and experience to realize how to apply the general principles of good practice to the specifics of her classroom. Once again, this brings to the fore the importance of good professional development for teachers and the need to let them experiment and learn from their experience.

I have taken all these lessons from the research literature seriously and have applied them in my own teaching. The results have been extremely gratifying to me and make me regret that earlier generations of my students did not benefit from my later knowledge of what makes for a more meaningful learning experience. But when I talk about my experiences to groups of teachers, I get some interesting responses.

I once gave a talk about my teaching strategies to the faculty at one of the leading large state universities. During the question period after my talk, one faculty member said that while he could see the value of what I said, he was skeptical about the general applicability of my methods. After all, he pointed out, I taught at a fairly selective private university (true), while he taught at a state university where they had to pretty much take anyone who met the low minimum entrance requirements. Hence, he said, I was probably working with a much "better" group of students and could expect them to do things he could not expect of his students.

This comment might have carried more weight with me were it not for the fact that some of my colleagues in my own, presumably selective, university were constantly complaining about how our students were not really interested in learning. The really good students, it was alleged, were going to even more selective universities, such as those of the Ivy League. Meanwhile, I have heard complaints from faculty at those very same elite universities that the students they get are those who are not necessarily focused on learning but are very good at taking tests and are highly grade focused. Such students, it is asserted, are willing to work hard to get a high grade but are not willing to take risks with learning or go deeply into the subject. (Recall the story of the AP student "Jeff" in chapter 2.)

But to close the circle, when I talk with teachers in urban school districts, they say they would be delighted to have a classroom full of the very kinds of students who are scorned by faculty at the elite colleges, students who are willing to work very hard just for the sake of a grade.

It seems that wherever and whomever they teach, teachers yearn for "better" students. I have come to the conclusion that all of us teachers believe in a glorious myth: out there, somewhere, there exists an ideal group of hardworking, intrinsically motivated students. If only we could get that group of students into our classrooms, our teaching problems would be solved. In other words, we could all be great teachers if only we had better students. This myth is probably part of a larger class of myths (e.g., that we could be better husbands if we had better wives, that we could be better parents if we had better children, that we could be better employers if we had better employees, and vice versa) that seeks to place the responsibility for any failure on the other party to the relationship.

The reality is that the only students we have are the ones in front of us in the classroom, and we could do a lot better with them if we took to heart the research on what makes for better learning and applied it. John Biggs supports this view when he says that "student motivation is a product of good teaching and not a prerequisite to it."

What kinds of strategies do we need to adopt in order to achieve the goals of improving education? The research is quite clear on this point. It has been stated before but is well worth repeating. We need well-structured cooperative-learning classrooms. We need hands-on, inquiry-based instruction. We need challenging curricula with support and guidance to enable students to achieve the specified goals. These strategies, grouped under the heading of "active learning," are all demonstrably effective in increasing learning.

How these broad guidelines are implemented in specific classrooms can be highly variable. It will depend on the age of the students, the subject taught, the size of the class, and the resources available. There are no universal prescriptions that can be applied across the board, so those looking for a quick fix to the problems of education will be disappointed. Instead, we are faced with the need to create teachers who have good content knowledge, who are connoisseurs of education and teaching, who know how to adapt to the immediate needs of their teaching situation, and who have a wide repertoire of teaching skills at their command and know which ones to call upon and apply in any given teaching situation. This is why ongoing, high-quality, professional-development programs for teachers are so crucial.

To reiterate the main points of this chapter, good teaching matters, and efforts should be directed toward creating a cadre of excellent teachers. Good teachers are made, not born, though clearly some arrive at the profession further along the path of excellence than others. The key to developing good teachers is the creation of ongoing, long-term, high-quality, professional-development programs in a school atmosphere that allows them room and time for reflection; consultation with peers and specialists; freedom to take risks in innovations, with the possibility of failing so that they can learn and improve; and freedom from tight external controls in the form of too-close supervision and direction, high-stakes proficiency testing, and rigid and overburdened curricula. While teachers should not be tightly constrained by curricula, they do need clear goals and standards at benchmark levels.

It has to be realized that exhortations to strive for excellence are not enough, and good intentions and idealism on the part of teachers are also not enough. We should also avoid the trap of looking for teacher charisma as though there is some mystical quality that good teachers possess that enables them to be successful. To be sure, some elements of teacher personality are important. A teacher who is a misanthrope or lacks respect for students is unlikely to ever succeed. But I believe that anyone who believes that learning can and should be enjoyable and who treats students with dignity and respect can become a good teacher.

As stated at the beginning of this chapter, the conclusion that good teaching matters for student learning will strike many as so obvious as to be not worth stating. And so it should be. But we do not *act* as if it were obvious. If we really thought so, then the continuous professional development of teachers, especially those new to the profession, would be at the forefront of all educational-reform efforts. It should use our best knowledge of what makes students want to learn to provide new teachers with the kinds of mentoring, training, and feedback that take them from novice teachers to the kind of skilled professionals who can have a transforming effect on students. This cannot be achieved quickly or cheaply.

NOTES

1. Ronald F. Ferguson, "Teachers' Expectations and the Test Score Gap," in *The Black–White Test Score Gap*, ed. Christopher Jencks and Meredith Phillips (Washington, DC: Brookings Institution Press, 1998), 273–317.

2. Kati Haycock, "Closing the Achievement Gap," *Educational Leadership* (March 2001): 6–11.

3. Regina Brett, "The Race for Proficiency," *The Plain Dealer Sunday Magazine* (22 June 2003): 8–17.

4. Ferguson, "Teachers' Expectations," 273–317.

5. Ferguson, "Teachers' Expectations," 273–317.

6. Ferguson, "Teachers' Expectations," 273–317.

7. Ferguson, "Teachers' Expectations," 273–317.

8. Ferguson, "Teachers' Expectations," 273–317.

9. Ferguson, "Teachers' Expectations," 273–317.

10. Maryellen Weimer, *Learner-Centered Teaching* (San Francisco: Jossey-Bass, 2002), 74–76.

11. Virginia Richmond and James McCroskey, *Power in the Classroom* (Hillsdale, NJ: Lea, 1992).

12. John D. Bransford, Ann L. Brown, and Rodney R. Cocking, eds., *How People Learn* (Washington, DC: National Academy Press, 1999).

13. Bransford, Brown, and Cocking, *How People Learn*, 106.

14. James E. Zull, *The Art of Changing the Brain* (Sterling, VA: Stylus Publishing, 2002).

15. Zull, *The Art of Changing the Brain*, 108.

16. John T. Bruer, "The Mind's Journey From Novice to Expert: If We Know the Route, We Can Help Students Negotiate Their Way," *American Educator* (Summer 1993): 6–15, 38–46.

17. Bransford, Brown, and Cocking, *How People Learn*, 20–30.

18. Bransford, Brown, and Cocking, *How People Learn*, 29.

19. Bransford, Brown, and Cocking, *How People Learn*, 30.

20. Bransford, Brown, and Cocking, *How People Learn*, 35

21. Bransford, Brown, and Cocking, *How People Learn*, 44.

22. Lion F. Gardiner, "Redesigning Higher Education: Producing Dramatic Gains in Student Learning," *ASHE-ERIC Higher Education Reports* 23, no. 7 (Washington, DC, 1996).

23. Bransford, Brown, and Cocking, *How People Learn*, 46.

24. Bransford, Brown, and Cocking, *How People Learn*, 59.

25. Bransford, Brown, and Cocking, *How People Learn*, 34.

26. See the Benezet Center Web site at www.inference.phy.cam.ac.uk/sanjoy/benezet.

27. Ronald F. Ferguson, "Can Schools Narrow the Black–White Test Score Gap?," in *The Black–White Test Score Gap*, ed. Jencks and Phillips, 318–74.

28. Alfie Kohn, *Punished by Rewards* (Boston: Houghton Mifflin, 1993).

29. Ferguson, "Teachers' Expectations," 273–317.

30. Kohn, *Punished by Rewards*.

31. Lillian McDermott, "What We Teach and What Is Learned—Closing the Gap," *American Journal of Physics*, 59 (1991): 301–15.

32. http://honolulu.hawaii.edu/intranet/committees/FacDevCom/guidebk/teachtip/7princip.htm.

33. F. Marton and R. Säljö, "On Qualitative Differences in Learning—I: Outcome and Process," *British Journal of Educational Psychology* 46 (1976): 4–11; and "On Qualitative Differences in Learning—II: Outcome as a Function of the Learner's Conception of the Task," *British Journal of Educational Psychology* 46 (1976): 115–27.

34. John Biggs, *Teaching for Quality Learning at University* (Buckingham UK: Society for Research in Higher Education and Open University Press, 1999), chap. 2.

35. Biggs, *Teaching for Quality Learning at University*, 4.

36. S. A. Cohen, "Instructional Alignment: Searching for a Magic Bullet," *Educational Researcher* 16, no. 8 (1987): 16–20; Bransford, Brown, and Cocking, *How People Learn*, 139; Biggs, *Teaching for Quality Learning at University*, 25–29.

37. D. W. Johnson, R. T. Johnson, and K. Smith, *Active Learning: Cooperation in the College Classroom* (Edina, MN: Interaction Book Company, 1991), 5:1–9.

38. Bransford, Brown, and Cocking, *How People Learn*, 47.

39. Johnson, Johnson, and Smith, *Active Learning*, 5:1–9.

40. Kohn, *Punished by Rewards*.

41. Paul R. Pintrich, "A Motivational Science Perspective on the Role of Student Motivation in Learning and Teaching Contexts," *Journal of Educational Psychology* 95, no. 4 (2003): 667–86; Martin V. Covington and Sonja Wiedenhaupt, "Turning Work into Play," in *Effective Teaching in Higher Education*, ed. Raymond P. Perry and John C. Smart (New York: Agathon Press, 1997), 101–14.

42. *Wall Street Journal* reporter Tara Parker-Pope, reprinted in the *Plain Dealer*, 6 January 2004, E3.

43. Bransford, Brown, and Cocking, *How People Learn*, 144.

44. David A. Kolb, *Experiential Learning* (Englewood Cliffs, NJ: Prentice-Hall, 1984).

45. Leonard Springer, Mary Elizabeth Stanne, and Samuel S. Donovan, "Effects of Small-Group Learning on Undergraduates in Science, Mathematics, Engineering, and Technology: A Meta-Analysis," National Institute for Science Education, Research Monograph no. 11, December 1997.

46. David W. Johnson, Roger T. Johnson, and Karl A. Smith, "Cooperative Learning Returns to College," *Change* 30, no. 4 (July/August 1998): 27.

9

WHY GOOD TEACHING PRACTICES ARE RELATIVELY RARE IN U.S. SCHOOLS AND EVEN RARER IN POOR AND MINORITY SCHOOLS

It is not hard to understand why good teaching reduces the size of the achievement gap. What happens in the classroom is extremely important, both in terms of what the teacher does and of the relationship that is created between teacher and student. I have argued in previous chapters that good teaching does not lie in the use of some particular set of curricular materials, or even in a particular set of personality traits.

Good teaching consists of those teaching methods that create in the minds of the learner a desire to learn. It is such teaching that can reduce or eliminate the achievement gap. We have seen that the conditions under which the desire to learn flourishes are those in which students have considerable autonomy and control over their learning, where inquiry-based learning techniques are used, and where students mostly work together cooperatively (and less frequently individually or competitively), and where they use hands-on, active-learning methods.

Such classrooms are more likely to have smaller achievement gaps. Conversely, classrooms that are authoritarian, primarily competitive, lecture-driven, and passive are more likely to result in larger achievement gaps.

A disturbing analysis by Kati Haycock and her colleages shows that in general, when it comes to science at least, black students receive a disproportionate amount of poor teaching.[1] Compared with eighth-grade white students, black students are twice as likely to have teachers who place little emphasis on developing laboratory skills, four times as likely to be assessed using hands-on activities only once or less per grading period, twice as likely to have a science teacher who does not emphasize development of data-analysis skills, three times as likely to engage in hands-on activities less than twice a month, less likely to have a teacher who participated in professional development the previous year, much less likely to have a certified teacher who has subject-matter competency, four times as likely to have rooms with little or no access to running water or a laboratory, and much less likely to have all the necessary materials.

The fact that such enormous disparities exist in the quality of teaching is hard to justify. After all, the United States is one of the richest countries in the world. It also has a high level of formal education, with about a quarter of its population having bachelor's degrees. This can enable schools to require that all teachers have such degrees, and in fact many teachers also have postgraduate degrees. Thus the formal education possessed by the teaching cadre in the United States is on a par with, or better than, that of teachers anywhere in the world. So why is there so much poor teaching?

In explaining this seeming anomaly, the first thing to realize is that good teaching practices are not learned through the formal education system that trains and certifies teachers. Of course the system equips teachers with some of the basic knowledge, tools, and skills, but formal education only gets you in the door, and it gives you a chance to prove yourself. Real expertise in any profession is developed through learning experiences encountered while practicing the profession. This is as true for teaching as it is for the practice of, say, medicine or law.

So what would it take for a novice teacher to develop the kind of knowledge and skills (outlined in the previous chapter) that make her into a seasoned professional, able to give her students the kinds of learning experiences that enable them, regardless of their ethnic and other differences, to learn at the highest levels?

The research indicates that it would require better *pre*-service training with a strong content-knowledge emphasis, ongoing support and professional development during the *in*-service years, more teacher autonomy, and less central control and direction. It takes about *10* years of sustained support and professional development (collaborative study, observation, curricular knowledge, and lesson refinement as part of their ongoing daily responsibilities) for beginning teachers to become accomplished professionals. This is true in the K–12 sector as well as for college teachers.[2]

But unfortunately this rarely happens. What new teachers usually get are the scattershot, single-session, workshop-style programs that pass for professional development in so many school districts. New teachers are hired and placed in classrooms and effectively left to fend for themselves. Teachers in both K–12 and college classrooms seem to be subjected to a kind of quiet social Darwinism in the belief that those who have the "right stuff" will succeed and stay on, while those who lack it will leave the profession. As a result of this benign neglect, most teachers never get the opportunity to develop into skilled practitioners. This attitude is in contrast to most other professions, where the care taken in hiring a new employee is usually followed up by ongoing training to help the new recruit learn from his or her subsequent job experiences and thus develop into a seasoned professional able to cope with a wide range of situations.

Another factor that works against good teaching is the increased use of high-stakes standardized testing and the so-called accountability movement, culminating in the No Child Left Behind legislation. This movement is based on plausible premises. It asserts that all children should be able to learn at high levels (true) and that all teachers should be able to teach well (also true). It then argues that the reason this is not happening is that students and teachers alike are not playing their respective roles effectively.

To correct for this, the accountability movement advocates the widespread and repeated testing of all students, and sometimes teachers. The results of this testing are then used to evaluate the performance of students, teachers, and schools. Schools and teachers that do not perform up to expectations are then subjected to sanctions. Accountability advocates argue that this will result in higher levels of achievement.

For those people committed to a behaviorist model of rewards and threats as the driving factors in human motivation, this makes sense. This model assumes that we can prod and push people to learn more by applying a judicious mix of external forces. But a little thought will show that high-stakes testing is bound to fail because of its own internal contradictions. In fact, the higher the stakes, the lower the level of real educational achievement, although test scores might rise.

It should be emphasized that there is nothing wrong with setting high curriculum standards that can be used as benchmarks for learning. Such standards are in fact desirable because they give teachers, parents, and students a better sense of what they should be aiming for.[3] The problems arise when the standards are used in a punitive way, by basing high-stakes *tests* on them and rewarding and punishing people based on those test results. Political realities immediately conspire to work against the professed goals.

The reasons for this are not hard to understand. Testing standards are necessarily set either by elected officials or by education department officials appointed by elected officials. These groups cannot set challenging assessments or standards for passing that are too high because if the tests result in a large number of student failures, these officials would soon have a vast number of angry parents swooping down on them and sweeping them from office. The No Child Left Behind legislation sets penalties for schools that do not do well on proficiency tests or do not meet improvement goals. So the pass rate has to be set at a level that is politically sustainable, as opposed to one that is based on purely educational grounds.

For example, the Ohio Board of Education initially set the passing scores for its new tenth-grade graduation test at 55 percent for reading and at 57 percent for mathematics. But the results of a trial run using this scale resulted in 66 percent of students passing reading and only 24 percent passing mathematics. Given that students had to pass tests in *all* five subjects they took (mathematics, reading, writing, science, and social studies), it was not hard to see that retaining the old passing-score bar would result in large numbers of students not meeting graduation requirements, mainly due to their failing in mathematics. The Board of Education knew there would be a huge outcry from enraged parents if their children failed to graduate. So in June 2004, the board reduced the passing scores to 42 percent correct for reading and 41 percent correct for mathematics. The new grading scale improves the situation considerably, with about 78 percent of students passing reading and 68 percent passing mathematics. Ohio is hardly alone in doing this kind of thing. Texas and Michigan had already made similar downward revisions in their passing standards.[4]

Compounding this kind of problem is the tendency of the media to use the aggregate test scores of districts to rate and rank them, putting pressure on "failing" schools to improve their scores. Thus individual school districts also have a vested interest in lowering standards because it does not do local school boards, superintendents, and other administrators any good to have large numbers of their own students failing the tests. So they exert pressure on the test implementers to ensure that the standards are not too high.

The philosophy underlying the accountability movement is the old carrot-and-stick one that has already been examined and found wanting. It is based on a very distorted and pessimistic view of learning. It is best captured in a 1991 cartoon by Camuso in which a little boy sits at a small desk looking bemused. Towering over him is a tank with the gun pointed directly at him. Seated in the turret of the tank, aiming the gun, is the self-styled "Education President," George H. W. Bush, looking sternly at the child and commanding him to "LEARN!"

As I have argued, real learning cannot be forced. We can force people to be very busy doing what we want them to do, but we cannot make students *want* to learn or make teachers *want* to teach well.

Another problem with the accountability movement and its emphasis on ranking school districts based on proficiency-test scores is that local bodies exert pressure on building principals to improve their test scores so that parents will feel that their children are going to good schools. These principals then exert pressure on classroom teachers to improve the scores of their students, and teachers end up teaching to the test and nothing but the test. As I have said earlier, "teaching to the test" is not in itself a bad thing. If the learning goals are sound, if the teaching practices used to achieve those goals are worthy, and if the assessments used to measure learning are meaningful, then teaching to the test can be very good. In fact, one should do exactly that because this is what is meant by a properly aligned curriculum. But high-stakes testing rarely leads to that result.

Most standardized testing occurs in a hopelessly unaligned educational framework where the learning goals are only loosely related to the tests.

Furthermore, the immense logistical issues that arise in repeatedly testing large numbers of students require that the tests be easily and quickly
gradable, preferably by machines. Also, when you have high-stakes tests,
the pressure is on the test designers to be able to withstand challenges
from aggrieved parents and schools that they are unfair, subjective, or biased. All these pressures conspire toward the creation of tests that measure low-level "objective" factoids in a multiple-choice format. In such
cases, teaching to the test results in basically force-feeding students with
facts in the weeks prior to the test. It is not unusual for school districts in
Ohio to spend the weeks before the proficiency-test dates doing nothing
but drilling students for the test. A teacher once told me that after the
test was over in early May, her class asked her why they still had school.
From the point of view of her students, the huge emphasis on preparing
for the test had convinced them that the whole point of coming to school
was to take the test. Once that was over, the students felt that there was
nothing else to be done, nothing more to be learned.

Good performances on standardized tests and other traditional assessments may not indicate real learning. But a focus on genuine learning can
lead to better performance on standard assessments because it gives students the ability to figure out for themselves what they need to know and
how to acquire that knowledge. My own experience with undergraduate
physics education is illustrative. Most students come to college physics
courses with the idea that physics consists of a large number of formulas
and an even larger number of problems, and that learning physics means
learning which formula to apply to solve which problem. It is basically a
match-the-formula-to-the-problem puzzle. They tend to dislike physics
for this reason, which is hardly surprising.

I decided that one of my main teaching goals was to disabuse students
of this notion and that my role was to teach physics in a way that enabled
students to understand the underlying principles and philosophy of
physics, to give students insight into how physicists view the world and
into the kinds of tools physicists use in interpreting the world. They
should be able to see that it was not necessary to remember all the formulas that once burdened them. All they really needed to learn were a
few fundamental laws, and, if they really understood how those laws
worked, they would have the keys to unlock the world of physics problems that had so intimidated them. Since I was usually teaching students

who were going to be either engineers or science majors, and since they did not have to take entrance exams in physics to get into these programs, I had the freedom to make choices about what to teach, how to teach, and what to assess. So I taught them what I thought was important and assessed them on it.

But I remember the first time I was asked to teach the physics course sequence that aspiring medical students have to take. In designing the course, I wondered what physics a doctor might need to know to practice his or her profession well. I called the curriculum director of a medical school and asked him what physics he would like his incoming medical students to know. There was a long pause as the question sank in, and then he replied that he did not know but would find out. But I already suspected that I knew the answer and was not surprised when he never called back. From the point of view of the medical school, physics was just a box that had to be checked off in the list of premedical courses that had to taken by all aspiring physicians. Perhaps in the distant past somebody had given some thought to what physics a doctor should know and had made a list of topics and skills that was passed on to physics departments. But over time, needs change, and subject disciplines change also, and course curricula become increasingly estranged from their original purpose. New topics are regularly added to syllabi, but rarely are any old ones removed, resulting in the current state of highly dense syllabi that require a lot of material be delivered. This results in a bias favoring the lecture format of instruction, which allows for rapid information transmission.

This is not unusual or peculiar to premedical physics courses. This is a standard result for courses that are seen as "service" courses, taught primarily to prepare people to take other courses, or for courses that are not driven by the interests of the instructor but are prepared by committees to serve some general interest. Such curricula inevitably grow over time as each subsequent instructor feels obliged to teach the "core" but also wants to add things that he or she feels are new or interesting or important. This creates a larger "core" for the next instructor, so we end up with curricula that are large and unwieldy and lack any kind of coherent purpose.

I remember Arnold Arons of the University of Washington, author of several classic books and articles on the teaching of physics,[5] telling a group of college faculty that when he was asked to teach the introductory physics sequence, he decided to only teach the core ideas that he thought were important, along with the skills and the thinking patterns that were necessary for a deep understanding of those ideas. He brutally eliminated all topics in the committee-designed curricula that did not meet these criteria. I asked him if he did not receive complaints from faculty members who taught these same students downstream when the students did not know some topic that was in the "official" syllabus but that he had eliminated. He replied that no one even noticed the drastic changes in content he had introduced, although some remarked that they were surprised by the depth of some of the questions that students had begun asking.

Heartened by my recollection of Arons's words, I decided to adopt the same strategy for my premed physics course. But I did have an additional constraint. The premeds had to eventually take a high-stakes, standardized, Medical College Admission Test (MCAT) and do well on that test in order to get into medical school. Since that test was out of my control, I wondered whether I should look carefully at those tests and teach to them or continue with my preferred philosophy of teaching for understanding.

I decided against "teaching to the (MCAT) test" based on my belief that students are smart and that if they learn the key ideas in any subject at a deep level, they can, when they need it, learn anything specific that they need for a specific purpose. I shared this philosophy with my students, telling them what my teaching strategy was going to be. In my subsequent interactions with students after they had completed my course and taken the MCAT, I asked them whether they felt at all disadvantaged in preparing for that high-stakes test. They replied that when they were preparing for it, they understood the foundations of physics well enough that they were able to learn on their own those details that I did not teach them in order to do well on the MCAT.

The point of these anecdotes is to emphasize my belief that even the overbearing presence of standardized tests does not mean that we have to teach at a low level to these tests. If we focus on good teaching that leads to deep learning, students can learn what they need for specific purposes, if they wish to learn. As teachers, the most we can do is try and create in our students the desire to learn and provide them with the overall conceptual framework and learning skills that will enable them to learn on their own. We cannot *make* them learn.

But in order to do this, teachers need some freedom and autonomy in determining what and how to teach their subjects, and they will need the time to teach well. These conditions still exist to some extent in the college sector (though not all instructors take full advantage of it), but they are sorely lacking in the K–12 sector. In K–12 classrooms, teachers are being increasingly straitjacketed with highly dense curricula and high-stakes testing of lower-level knowledge and skills, leaving them with fewer and fewer opportunities to practice the creative art of teaching. Nowhere is the distorting effect of an overwrought curriculum on teaching more visible than in the advanced-placement (AP) curriculum and tests.

A report commissioned by the National Research Council, for example, stated that "the Physics Panel concluded that the current AP Physics B course . . . includes too many disparate topics to allow most high-school students to achieve an adequate level of conceptual understanding. . . . Because of the high stakes and potential benefits of AP examinations, too often it is the examinations, rather than educational goals, that drive the instructional process. Students will generally do what is necessary to score well on examinations, and their teachers will generally assist those efforts."[6]

In my own children's high school, for example, one of the most gifted teachers is a U.S. history teacher. As a result of his reputation, his AP U.S. history class enrolls the highest achievers among the students, students who are focused and willing to work very hard. But at the open house with parents, this teacher ruefully said that the AP curriculum is so dense that he would have to focus on the actual events of history that were required by the test and hence would have little time left over to explore with his class the way that current events illuminate, and are illuminated by, the study of history. This latter feature is what really makes history so fascinating and relevant as a subject. But this superior approach had to be abandoned in order to get students ready to answer the questions on the AP test. As a colleague of mine wryly says about the required pacing of U.S. history courses, if the curriculum is going to be "covered," then "whatever else might happen, Sherman has to be in Atlanta by Thanksgiving." Despite this tight constraint, my children's history teacher had the superior skills to still make the AP U.S. history course interesting. But he could have done a lot more if he had the freedom and flexibility to do so. Less competent teachers, however, will adopt a "just the facts" approach that serves nobody well, although it might result in good test results.

High-stakes testing negatively affects both subject-matter content and instruction.[7] The tendency of high-stakes proficiency testing to drive curriculum and teaching for the worse is widespread. There seems to be a version of Gresham's law that applies in education in which bad teaching drives out the good.

I recall an experience with school principals in the Cleveland school district that illustrates my point. During the 1990s, I was involved for many years with Project Discovery, the state of Ohio's National Science Foundation's Statewide Systemic Initiative to improve mathematics and science education. In that program, we worked with teachers to increase their use of active, hands-on, inquiry-based, cooperative methods of learning. In such classrooms, students were encouraged to experiment and to discuss and argue hypotheses with one another and the teacher.

While the teachers in the program were enthusiastic about these methods of teaching and could see their advantages for better learning, they were apprehensive about whether they would be able to fully implement them once they returned to their own classrooms because such methods require time to implement, and dense curricular requirements might work against them. What the teachers reported back to us was that an unanticipated problem had arisen. Their building principals did not understand this new method of teaching in which students are encouraged to move around, talking with one another, as they worked to solve challenging problems. This went against the traditional model of a "good" classroom in which the students sit quietly in neat rows and listen to the teacher. The active-learning classroom struck these principals as one in which the teacher had lost control, and teachers were being discouraged from teaching in this way for fear of poor appraisals. Teachers found it hard to continue in such a nonsupportive atmosphere.

In order to counteract this, Project Discovery created a separate program for principals in the Cleveland schools, where we introduced them to the nature of active learning in mathematics and science and what such a classroom would look like so they would be more understanding and appreciative of what their teachers were doing. The program was going well as the principals (many of whom recounted how they themselves as students had hated mathematics and science classes) experienced for themselves the enjoyment of learning in this different way. For many, it was a revelation in how to teach.

But one day a speaker was invited at short notice to replace a regularly scheduled presenter. This new speaker showed the group a set of mathematics flash cards that had various mathematics "facts." The speaker asserted that drilling students with these flash cards would increase students' mathematics proficiency scores by a few points. I watched in horror as the principals seized on this chance to raise test scores, even if by a small amount. Although this method of teaching sacrifices higher-level learning skills (which would help students in the long run) by replacing them with memorization, the principals were eager to adopt it. Anything that improved test scores had great appeal to them, even if it discouraged long-term higher-level learning skills and produced only short-term benefits on low-level cognitive measures.

One could sympathize with the principals' plight. Their jobs were often on the line, held hostage to proficiency-test scores. Principals (as well as teachers and superintendents) are under constant pressure to improve the scores of the students in their building. No one ever asks them about the *quality* of the learning that is occurring. No one ever asks them if their students are enthusiastic about learning or about coming to school. Only the test scores seem to matter. Hence it was easy for them to rationalize that it was worthwhile abandoning methods that led to deeper learning in exchange for a few points' increase for some students. The pressure they felt to raise scores trumped any arguments that the long-term learning of students should be our primary goal as educators.

Commercial publishers are quick to take advantage of this pressure to improve test scores. In fact, the *Wall Street Journal* reports that if there are any winners at all in the accountability movement's push for high-stakes testing, it is the business sector (test publishers, tutoring services, teacher-training outfits, etc.) as they rush to provide services to supposedly failing schools.[8] They market curricula, programs, textbooks, or other materials (such as flash cards) that are supposedly "teacher-proof," in that they can be used to teach in recipe form by almost anyone. It is my opinion that there is no such thing as a teacher-proof curriculum. The centrality of the teacher in the learning process cannot be overestimated. In fact, the role of the teacher becomes even more important as we move toward active-learning methods that, at least superficially, seem to put more of the onus for learning on the student. It takes a very skilled teacher to make students realize that only they can learn, to create in them the desire to learn, and to provide students with the learning skills and resources that enable them to do so.

In this way, high-stakes proficiency tests that measure low-level learning are the enemies of any attempt to make learning more meaningful, enjoyable, and worth doing for its own sake. And the pressure gets worse as the stakes get higher. The increased emphasis on test taking and accountability results in lower academic achievement as everyone conspires to undermine the tests in order to not be held accountable. The shenanigans do not end with simply bad teaching, as harmful as that is. It is inevitable that teachers and school administrators will be tempted to resort to various dubious, nonacademic strategies to raise scores. These could involve outright cheating (such as giving students the answers to test questions or changing student answers), administrative ruses such as excluding those students at high risk of failing the tests by labeling them as learning disabled (thus eliminating them from the ranks of test takers), or even temporarily expelling these students from school on trumped up charges so that they are not included in the test statistics. These and other devices have been reported from time to time.[9]

The typical response to such attempts to circumvent the goals of testing and accountability is to impose more rules, have more watchdogs, and impose closer supervision and scrutiny. The more this is done, the more resources will be diverted away from actual teaching and into rule enforcement. And we will have an even more controlling environment for both teachers and students and a further devaluing of the sense of professionalism of teachers as they find monitors constantly peering over their shoulders.

This whole mind-set is based on the assumption that teachers and students will not do their best work unless forced to do so. But this assumption is false. Learning is a creative process and, like all creative processes, flourishes in an atmosphere of freedom and lack of rules. Consider the conditions under which writers and painters and sculptors work. They cannot be forced to produce their best creations by making them adhere to a rigid schedule. The best results come about when artists are allowed a great deal of leeway in how and when they do their work.

We seem to have come to think of learning as if it were similar to digging ditches. We can probably get excellent ditches by forcing people to dig ditch after ditch to precise specifications and rewarding them for succeeding and punishing them for failing. (The film *Holes* provides a good example of this.) People would probably get very good at this task, but as soon as you stop forcing them to dig or take away the rewards for meeting exact specifications, the ditch diggers will stop working. They will not want to dig ditches for its own sake.

But with learning, we *do* want people to continue learning even when no one is looking, when there is no reward. That is what the lifelong-learning philosophy is all about. But by emphasizing the carrot-and-stick approach to learning, we are ensuring that this will not occur. After all, the implicit message of giving students rewards for learning, or threatening them with failure, is that we think learning is not worth doing for its own sake and that no one would do it unless forced to. After many years of experiencing this in schools, should it be surprising that students have such a negative view of learning and school?

Think of the happiness with which students look forward to weekends or the summer holidays when they do not have to go to school. Think of the glee with which students greet an unexpected school closing like a snow day. Children even fantasize about some catastrophe that will shut school down. We have come to think of such a reaction as normal. We would be really concerned with a student's mental state if she was disappointed that school was closed or if she approached the summer with sadness as she realized that there would be no more scheduled learning experiences.

That we have come to think of school as being similar to an unfulfilling job with its "thank God it's Friday" mentality is a sign of how low our expectations have sunk when it comes to education. Even the world of work should not, at its best, have this negative connotation. Ideally people should find their employment so fulfilling that they look forward to Monday, or at least treat work as an important and fulfilling part of their lives. Looking at the causes of alienation in work is beyond the scope of this book, but there is no reason why we should accept this dismal attitude toward education as normal.

After all, most young children in elementary school, once they get over their separation anxiety about leaving their home and families, love to go to school. They see it as the place to experience things in the company of other children that they could not experience in their homes. How did we get so good at beating that attitude out of them so that by the time they reach middle school in a few years, they have come to think of school as a joyless place and learning as a chore? What would it take for us to build on that initial enthusiasm for school so that their love for learning grows with the years? Why don't we look at that as the fundamental challenge of education, not raising scores on some test?

For those people who are so wedded to tests that they cannot envisage learning without them, I can offer a compromise. We could devise measures to *assess students' love of learning* and focus our education efforts on improving scores on that particular measure. I predict that all the other, more traditional measures of learning will improve along with the desire to learn.

The added importance of this for children of poor and deprived homes cannot be emphasized enough. Children of affluent or even middle-class homes have access to informal and enjoyable educational experiences in their homes. The presence of newspapers, magazines, and books in their homes means that children have opportunities to read for fun. They are also stimulated by frequent contact with educated adults in a variety of professions who provide ideas that can informally enrich their experience of life and broaden their horizons. All these valuable learning experiences are not part of the regimented learning experience we call school.

The middle-class lifestyle also provides other beneficial effects due to the kinds of parenting practices that are common to that class. Informal learning experiences outside the home include trips to libraries, museums, community events, and grocery stores, and visits to friends. Literary experiences and other cognitively stimulating activities occur spontaneously within the home when the mother reads to a child, when a family member reads the newspaper, or when the family subscribes to magazines.[10]

But poor children have few of these advantages, and these differences in practices have a significant effect on scores.[11] The research indicates that it takes at least *two generations* for changes in parental socioeconomic status to exert their full effect on parenting practices. As we saw earlier, there are not many grounds for optimism that the socioeconomic divide will disappear any time soon. We cannot simply wait for these broader socioeconomic improvements to occur. The educational sector has to meet this challenge.

I am not saying that schools and teachers should take on the role of surrogate parents and families. Teachers are already burdened with too many nonteaching roles. But if teachers see their primary task as not purely that of teaching students knowledge and skills, but also appreciate the critical importance of developing an emotional investment in learning on the part of the child, then they would naturally, as part of their teaching strategy, incorporate many of the practices that middle-class children experience in their homes.

If, however, we see the role of teachers as being primarily cognitive-skill developers, then the achievement gap will remain because black students are not as committed to the threat-and-reward structure of present-day schooling as white children and their parents are. For black children, it is even more important that school be the place they look forward to, where they feel that they can grow intellectually, where they can work with their peers on challenging experiences, where the teacher is seen as their guide and friend who will help them learn better. School should be a stimulating place that awakens their curiosity, exposes them to a wide variety of experiences, and makes them want to develop the skills that will enable them to learn more.

It is tempting to dismiss this image of school as being hopelessly idealistic. For many people, even those who have become successful by conventional measures, school was at best an adequate place. They learned some knowledge and skills, they got credentials that helped them get into college or get jobs, but that was it. School is not looked back on as an exciting *learning* experience, although there may be some nostalgia for childhood in general. Such people cannot imagine school being anything better than it was for them. This is the real tragedy of the educational system today. We have lost sight of the fact that learning is one of the most natural and enjoyable experiences a person can have. Aristotle was right, but we don't believe him.

But we have to do better, if we are to close the achievement gap.

The last chapter of this book will look at some of the deep-seated roots of the problems of education and how we arrived at the present system. For the moment, I would like to examine the question of why change and improvement in schools seems so hard to achieve. Perhaps one of the most perceptive observers of why we have not been able to achieve positive change in schools is Seymour Sarason.[12]

Sarason points out that education is a complex, nonlinear system. It is not amenable to linear thinking, so you cannot resort to the usual solution strategy of creating a hierarchy, listing problems in order of importance, and solving them one at a time. Yet this is the strategy that is usually adopted. We try to identify the main source of the problem and focus on that and that alone. But in education there are many culprits, and it is hard to assess which ones are the most important. Trying to solve each problem piecemeal is futile because the massive combined inertia of the rest of the system works against any improvement in a single component.

Think of the components in the educational network as like the set of springs that make up a mattress. They are all tightly connected in a big network, each spring tightly constrained by its neighbors. In one sense, this is a strength of the system. If a single spring breaks, the rest can still effectively fill its role with only a slight loss in functionality. This explains why a seriously underperforming school system can limp along for a long time without actually ceasing to function. Teacher positions eliminated? Increase class sizes. Budgets cut? Eliminate arts, music, and busing. And so on. As long as we are focused on maintaining the superficial features of school and don't pay attention to whether students are developing a love of learning, the system can adapt to almost any adversity by making adjustments elsewhere.

But this same strength also makes the system difficult to change. Back to the mattress analogy, if we replace just one spring by a better one, the remaining spring system works in concert to prevent any substantive change from occurring due to that new spring.

The educational system also works this way. Any piecemeal reform in one area seems to have little effect because the problems in the other areas tend to suppress the benefits of that one reform, leading to the de-spairing conclusion that none of the explanations that have been gener-ated for the achievement gap seems to be the true one. This is because in nonlinear systems the sum can be more or less than its parts, and changes have to be implemented more holistically, with an appreciation for the fact that before any change can have its desired effect, we must take into account the other factors that impinge on that change and make accommodations for them as well. But if we try to change each component independently of the influence of others, we will seemingly find that the change has no effect. We are then tempted to dismiss the whole reform exercise as hopeless and go back to doing what we always did before, asserting that there is an unchangeable factor that is pre-venting improvement. It is this kind of faulty reductionist reasoning that led people like Murray and Herrnstein to arrive at seriously wrong con-clusions such as that genetic IQ differences must be the cause of the achievement gap.

For example, one common analysis of the problems in education (fa-vored by executives in the corporate world who see the business model as a suitable template for running the schools) is that the problem lies with the people in the school system, namely teachers and school ad-ministrators. It is asserted that these people either cannot or will not do their jobs properly, and the solution is to replace them with better peo-ple. If we could only get the "correct" or "best" people in these posi-tions, this line of thinking goes, the problem would be solved.

But which group is most in need of being replaced? My experience with teachers at all levels indicates that each group views the other with suspicion. College teachers tend to place the blame squarely on high school teachers. If only they (i.e., high school teachers) had done their jobs properly, then colleges would not need affirmative-action admission programs, would not have to do any remedial work, and could get on with the real business of teaching their students college-level material.

Oddly enough, high school teachers tend to say very similar things, but about middle school teachers. If only middle school teachers had done their job, they (the high school teachers) would be able to teach what they are supposed to and would prefer to, without spending so much time on remediation. And middle school teachers say the same things about elementary school teachers, who in turn blame parents and families and society because children do not come to school ready to learn. College teachers do not seem to realize that they are part of the problem too and are not exempt from blame, since they are the ones who educated the teachers to begin with. It seems that each segment of the educational system is hoping that changes *elsewhere* will solve the problems.

This kind of blame shifting is endemic. Teachers, building administrators, district administrators, school boards, and state and federal education policymakers all tend to blame each other for the failures of education. Each tends to propose changes in areas other than its own. All the suggestions are posed as "for the sake of the children." The truth is that we are all complicit in creating this problem.

In my work with teachers and administrators in various education systems, there is no question that I have encountered some people who really should be in another line of work. And no doubt there have been countless attempts to replace incompetent people with new recruits. But we should not forget that many people *choose* to go into education; they were not forced into it. And we have had many generations of teachers as fresh faces replace those who retire. There is no reason to think that the new people entering the teaching profession now are any more committed and idealistic than the current teaching cadres were when they began teaching. The real question that should be asked is not about how to replace poorly performing people but about why they become so. Instead of trying to get rid of this so-called deadwood, we should be asking what it is that is killing all the healthy trees in the forest.

In science, when an important, but seemingly soluble, problem resists solution, it is usually a sign that the problem has not been formulated correctly and that we are looking at it in the wrong way. Applying this principle to the achievement gap in education, the seeming intractability of the problem may be a sign that the current focus on the ✓ black–white gap is not correct. I have argued that we should instead focus on the gap between where *all* students are now and *where they should be*. We should not treat it as a black problem with white levels of achievement as the norm. We need to view the problem as one with the educational system as a whole and create awareness that the equity gap is a symptom of widespread educational failure. The overall performance of all groups leaves a lot to be desired, and we are simply not challenging our students as well as we should. As a result, the ones who have the least investment in the system and have the most viable *immediate* alternatives to school give up most easily, and we end up with the achievement gap. Punitive actions and remedial work make the situation even worse.

To return to the metaphor of the teacher as a gardener, a well-kept garden seems to grow by itself. The point is that it takes a great deal of skill on the part of the teacher to make himself or herself invisible in the learning process. It takes much less skill to play the traditional role of being a sage. But developing the skills of a master gardener takes time. This is why I feel that the best investment that a school district can make is in the ongoing professional development of its teaching faculty. This would require that school districts protect and even increase their professional-development budgets for teachers. But the sad fact is that in times of budget cuts, professional-development allocations tend to be among the first in line for cuts, and underachieving schools are the ones that are likely to have the least resources for this.

Good teaching focuses on enhancing students' natural desire to learn. This requires professional development more than equipment and supplies. A good teacher can teach more with bits of string, cardboard, and tape than an inferior teacher can with all the computers, equipment, textbooks, and supplies at their disposal. Poor teaching has a disproportionately negative effect on the performance of black students, and the educational achievement gap flows inexorably from this situation.

Readers of this book, who are likely to be among those people who feel that they have received a good education, may be wondering how it can be that they managed to succeed given the case that has been made that schools in general are not doing a good job of teaching. Arnold Arons argues that in his experience only a few students (about 25 percent) develop the kinds of critical-thinking skills and abstract-reasoning patterns that enable them to learn at higher levels, and that this breakthrough occurs *spontaneously* and not as a result of any planned educational program.[13]

Arons argues that such people became educated largely *despite* the teaching they received, not because of it, and warns them to avoid reading too much into their own success. "Casual extrapolation of one's own experience only leads to error. Those of us who are fortunate enough to have become competent professionals are among the 25 percent minority mentioned earlier. We made the breakthrough in spite of the system, not because of it. Our own learning experiences are not representative, and citing such experience rarely leads to correct insight into what transpires for the majority of learners."[14]

On the one hand, it is sad to think that Arons may well be right and that nearly all our teaching efforts are currently wasted. But if we want to see the glass as half full, it is also heartening in that it shows that a significant number of people can learn how to learn on their own. Imagine how much more can be achieved if the others had the correct kinds of guidance from teachers to enable them to rise to similar heights, highlighting once more the central role that teachers play. As Arons says, "I dwell so insistently on the teachers only because of the crucial role they play in sustaining the feedback loop. Think of the prodigious impetus that might stem from altering the condition of the teachers and making the feedback regenerative instead of degenerative."[15]

NOTES

1. Kati Haycock, Craig Jerald, and Sandra Huang, "Closing the Gap: Done in a Decade," *Education Trust: Thinking K–16* 5, no. 2 (Spring 2001).

2. John D. Bransford, Ann L. Brown, and Rodney R. Cocking, eds., *How People Learn* (Washington, DC: National Academy Press, 1999); Robert Boice, *Advice for New Faculty Members: Nihil Nimus* (Boston: Allyn and Bacon, 2000).

3. Jane Butler Kahle, Judith Meece, and Kathryn Scantlebury, "Urban African-American Middle School Students: Does Standards-Based Teaching Make a Difference?" *Journal of Research in Science Teaching* 37, no. 9 (2000): 1019–41.

4. Sam Dillon, "States Readjust Education Standards," *The Plain Dealer*, 22 May 2003, A4.

5. Arnold B. Arons, *A Guide to Introductory Physics Teaching* (New York: John Wiley and Sons, 1990).

6. Jerry P. Gollub and Robin Spital, "Advanced Physics in the High Schools," *Physics Today* 55, no. 5 (May 2002): 48.

7. Alfie Kohn, *The Case Against Standardized Testing: Raising the Scores, Ruining the Schools* (Portsmouth, NH: Heinemann, 2000).

8. June Kronholz, "'No Child' Law Proves a Boon to Businesses," *The Plain Dealer*, 27 December 2003, C3.

9. Education Trust Report, "Getting Away with It: What Happens When No One's Minding the Store," www2.edtrust.org/EdTrust/Press+Room/tell+the+truth.htm.

10. Meredith Phillips et al., "Family Background, Parenting Practices, and the Black-White Test Score Gap," in *The Black–White Test Score Gap*, ed. Christopher Jencks and Meredith Phillips (Washington, DC: Brookings Institution Press, 1998), 103–45.

11. Phillips et al., "Family Background," 103–45.

12. Seymour B. Sarason, *The Predictable Failure of Educational Reform* (San Francisco: Jossey-Bass, 1990).

13. Arons, *A Guide to Introductory Physics Teaching*, 324.

14. Arons, *A Guide to Introductory Physics Teaching*, 325.

15. Arons, *A Guide to Introductory Physics Teaching*, 324–25.

10

HOW AND WHY DID
IT GET THIS WAY?

In the last chapter, we saw that after just a few years of schooling, children seem to adopt a negative attitude toward school that is similar to what most people have toward work. School is seen as a chore. Weekends and holidays are looked forward to as opportunities to do what people really like, as opposed to weekdays, when people feel they are forced to do things decided by *other* people.

This close correspondence between student attitudes toward school and adult attitudes toward work is taken for granted as the normal state of affairs. A child who cried because he or she could *not* go to school because of a snow day or for some other reason would be considered quite strange. But such a similarity in attitudes should be quite surprising. After all, the two worlds are quite dissimilar. The world of work is driven, at least in America, largely by the needs of profit making, in which the needs and wants of the worker are secondary. Most owners and managers of businesses do not pay much attention to whether the work they require from their employees satisfies the workers' emotional and intellectual needs. It would be a truly unusual owner who routinely inquired of employees whether they were happy or who worried about whether the work they were asking their employees to do was interesting to them. As long as the worker does what he or she is expected to do without complaining, the employer is satisfied. The needs of the employees are met only in order to fulfill the requirements of the law and to prevent unrest or serious discontent that might prevent the smooth running of the enterprise.

Although this approach has been critiqued on the grounds that *in the long run* it makes for better business practices to deal with the overall well-being of workers, such an enlightened attitude is relatively rare among employers or is used only for upper-level management or those in jobs requiring high levels of creativity. In most cases, short-term profits are what many business owners and managers seek, since they seem to take to heart the dictum of economist John Maynard Keynes who said, "In the long run, we are all dead."

In such a controlling, profit-oriented environment, it makes sense to have employees who respond in predictable ways to external influences, such as rewards and threats. You need people who think that the only reason for working is to earn money and that the only issues to be concerned about are salary and benefits. Once employees have embraced this mind-set, they can be easily controlled using such levers, and the careful utilization of rewards (such as salary, benefits, bonuses, promotions, status, and other perks) and threats (mainly the prospect of being disciplined, demoted, or fired) in order to increase the productivity of such workers makes a kind of narrow sense.

But schools are very different from businesses. The profit motive is entirely absent. Their goals are (or at least should be) very long-term, since they should be trying to prepare students for their entire lives. The aim of schools is (or, again, should be) to provide an intellectually stimulating environment that also enhances the emotional well-being of students and emphasizes cooperative behavior. School should be the place that students delight in, that is the highlight of their day. So it should actually be astounding that the negative attitudes of workers toward their daily occupation should be reflected so accurately in the attitudes of students toward school. The fact that they are so similar should give us some pause. How could this happen? Could it be just a coincidence?

There are undoubtedly people who think that learning does involve suffering and that such a negative attitude toward school is wholly appropriate. I am going to ignore those with such a bleak attitude toward education.

Others might take a more generous view, agreeing with me that children should not have these negative attitudes toward school but concluding that this is a sign that a well-intentioned educational system has gone awry. It is to such people that this chapter is addressed.

I believe that a more realistic view is that such a remarkable congruence in peoples' attitudes toward school and work cannot be an accident but must be by design. This answer might be more apparent if we posed the question of what might happen if schools actually did succeed in their publicly stated fundamental educational goal and produced graduates who are knowledgeable and intellectually curious, think critically, see the world in big-picture terms, are willing to take risks, seek to understand why things are the way they are, are accomplished problem solvers, try to devise ways to make the world better for everyone, and act on their ideals and convictions. What if schools produced people who understand and appreciate the fundamental concepts of justice and freedom and democracy, and seek to implement these concepts in all aspects of their lives?

If schools produced such people, it would be a disaster for all those businesses that currently depend on the existence of a large pool of people who are willing to accept that it is their lot in life to work in dull, routine, low-paying jobs with little or no benefits in terms of health or retirement and no job security, while owners and senior managers have much better conditions. Without a large supply of such people, how would retailers such as Wal-Mart be able to provide the rest of us with low prices on their goods? How would fast-food outlets get the large numbers of employees for their low-paying jobs that enable the rest of us to purchase hamburgers so cheaply? How would hotels and restaurants get the low-paid cleaning personnel and waitstaff that enable the rest of us to afford to stay in those hotels and eat at those restaurants?

It is also important for business that these workers not feel a sense of solidarity with their fellow workers but instead feel that they are dependent on the goodwill of management and that thus it is important for them to ingratiate themselves with their supervisors. Such businesses also need their employees to see their world in narrow terms, with their own role as being to come to work on time and do what they are told.

The politically powerful corporations that make profits because of the awful working conditions of their employees cannot risk having any other educational system than the kind we currently have. Recall Martin Luther King's insight (quoted in chapter 3) that "depressed living standards for Negroes are not simply the consequence of neglect. . . . They are a structural part of the economic system in the United States. Certain industries and enterprises are based upon a supply of low-paid, under-skilled and immobile nonwhite labor. Hand assembly factories, hospitals, service industries, housework, agricultural operations using itinerant labor would suffer economic trauma, if not disaster, with a rise in wage scales." What is being argued here is that King's analysis extends well beyond the black community and applies equally well to the permanent underclass of all ethnicities.

If schools succeeded in their stated goal of educating all students at a high level, the world of work as we now know it could not function. I believe it would be replaced by something better, but that is not the issue here. The point is that the close correspondence between the world of work and that of school cannot be seen as a curious coincidence. It has to be understood as a subtle but deliberate policy result. Schools produce the large numbers of alienated people of low cognitive skills who respond in a Pavlovian fashion to threats and rewards because that is precisely the kind of worker our present society currently needs. Schools are the way they are because the world of work as presently constituted needs them to be that way.

When viewed through this lens, the working of schools suddenly makes a lot of sense. If we see the role of schools as being to staff the world of work at different levels, then the way we treat students and the attitudes that such approaches generate become a lot more understandable. Even the different ways that schools and colleges are stratified and function (from elite universities to community colleges, from wealthy suburban schools to poor urban schools) can be understood if we see their purpose as to produce different kinds of workers to fill different niches in the workplace.

I have visited urban schools with all their drab and bare environments. I have seen the playgrounds with little grass and few or no trees to alleviate the stark outlines of the buildings. The only grass visible is that which defiantly struggles to grow in the cracks in the asphalt. I have approached windowless buildings, walked past metal detectors, been looked over by security guards. It is interesting that I have always been treated well by the students in those buildings. But the whole *atmosphere* of the building gave me a sense of unease. What is sad is that this is the kind of atmosphere that some students experience day after day, year after year, and what they thus come to accept as "normal." The teachers and students are no different from those in any other school. But they have to deal daily with an oppressive milieu. What does that tell them about what to expect, tolerate, and accept when they go out in the world?

It is interesting to compare such schools with a suburban school district I visited that is not particularly atypical. The building is clean, spacious, airy, carpeted, and brightly painted, with framed artwork on the walls. There are big windows that look out on huge campus-like grounds and playing fields, and there are picnic tables under the trees. No metal detectors, no security guards, and no surveillance cameras were visible.

This kind of contrast is not surprising. The vast differences in school resources between rich and poor schools have been amply documented elsewhere, and this point does not need further belaboring. What struck me most forcibly, however, was a small feature. While I was visiting the suburban school, I suddenly heard music coming through the public-address system, and soon after, the students came out of their classrooms on their way to the next class. My host, seeing my surprise, said that they did not use bells (or buzzers) to signify the end of one class and the beginning of the next. Instead, the music began and continued for the four minutes that were allocated for the transition. When the music faded, that meant it was time for the next class to begin. He said that the school district did not want to use bells, since they were teaching children whose future in their expected world of work would not feature them. These children were not expected to enter the world of sweatshops, factories, or shift work where the ringing of bells and buzzers is used to signal a change in routine. They were expected to go into the professions or the managerial sector or to be captains of industry.

In that vignette is captured an important distinction. It was not appropriate or desirable to train these particular students to respond to bells. Furthermore, the students themselves were involved in selecting the music that was played each day. Hence, not only were they not being trained to jump to commands, but they were being trained to *give* those commands. It is hard not to feel that these students are being prepared for a very different life from those in the urban inner-city schools, and the different kinds of preparation being offered had nothing to do with the educational achievement of these students.

If one of the unstated functions of schools is to produce people who will conform to, and satisfy the needs of, the modern corporate state, then they should create a large number of people who value things like honesty, punctuality, obedience, and willingness to follow instructions without wanting to see the big picture, and who see themselves as not capable of greater things. On the cover of the cartoon book *School is Hell*, by Matt Groening[1] (the creator of the popular television program *The Simpsons*), a proto–Bart Simpson character is writing repeatedly on the blackboard as punishment, "I must remember to be cheerful and obedient." Finally, he gets angry and writes on the last line, "I must remember SCHOOL IS HELL," before running away. That cartoon sums up the results of the educational system today for the majority of students. We try to make students docile and happy, but we end up with them being frustrated with school and waiting to get out.

But not all students should be prepared to be equally docile and submissive. We also need to have a small (but still significant in number) group who will be the middle managers of the economy. These people need to have internalized the values of the corporate state and made it their own. They are the enforcers of rules, and they should see the rules as just and natural. These people have superior technical skills and feel that they are different from, and superior to, the low-level workers. You never find these people socializing with the custodial staff, for example. They occupy the professional or managerial niches and see their loyalties as lying with upper management, not with the lower-paid workers.

These people are also encouraged to think within the narrow range that conventional wisdom regards as respectable views, while having a self-image of themselves as freethinkers or even as radicals. They see the range of opinions on the editorial pages of the *New York Times* or the *Washington Post* or the *Wall Street Journal* as representing the boundaries of acceptable opinion and would not dream of taking a position that lies outside that range. Indeed they often cannot even conceive that reasonable viewpoints outside this range can exist. They are primarily technicians who tend to accept unquestioningly the justness of the present structure of society. They work for improvements within the parameters set down for them.

At the very top of this educational pyramid are those students who are prepared for elite positions. These are the select few who are encouraged to see the big picture, to see themselves as the makers and breakers of rules, naturally born to exercise authority over others, while still internalizing the fundamental idea that this is the way the world should be. Such people, by virtue of their inherited wealth, social standing, education, and connections, become the effective rulers of our society, but they are encouraged to think of themselves as possessing some rare, intrinsic quality that makes them so successful. Oddly enough, such people are often more likely to realize that there are other ways to do things and that there are other ways of organizing society. But since they are the ones who benefit most from the current state of affairs, they are unlikely to seek changes.

For many people in the United States, this image of contemporary society would be shocking and repulsive. It smacks of the kind of feudal, class-bound societies of Europe and Asia, completely foreign to the popular image of a classless, meritocratic America, where everyone is believed to start life with an equal chance of success, where it is said that any child can grow up to be president. The idea that schooling may be replacing birth or caste as a primary mechanism for assigning people to selected roles and attitudes in society will be highly repugnant. After all, school is popularly perceived as the great equalizer, not the great discriminator.

But if we view schools as serving the needs of business as presently constituted, the structure of inner-city schools makes sense. The metal detectors, the locked doors, the security systems and guards, the humiliating lack of privacy and trust, the spy cameras, the appalling bathrooms with their lack of cleanliness and sometimes even doors, the rigid adherence to rules, the lack of freedoms, the absence of challenging self-directed curricula, the bare surroundings are all playing a role in conditioning the students who attend such schools to the kind of work life they are supposed to accept unquestioningly as natural. Students who grow up in such surroundings are already primed to accept similar surveillance, bleak environments, and lack of privacy and trust in their work lives. We may justify some of these harsh features on grounds of security for the students, teachers, and administrators in the buildings (and those reasons may well be valid), but we have to realize that they serve other roles as well.

It is interesting that although poor urban schools are always short of money for educational supplies and professional development for high-quality teacher training, money is always found to serve coercive goals. High-quality schools and skilled teachers that can create the conditions that make students want to learn are less likely to need the prison-like atmosphere that is supposed to make people feel safer. But such measures are unlikely to be funded because they will not be serving the other, hidden, need of reconciling large numbers of students to a lower quality of life.

In fact, it is always interesting to look at what education programs get cut and what get funded in times of budget shortfalls. When schools run short of money, the first items to be eliminated are the music and arts programs, extracurricular activities such as student clubs and societies, and sports. Such decisions are defended on the grounds that the fundamentals (reading, mathematics, and science) have to be preserved. Such arguments are not without merit, and as a scientist myself, I fully support maintaining these academic programs. But it is also true that it is in the music, arts, clubs, societies, and sports that students are freed from excessive authority and routine, learn leadership and teamwork, and have outlets for creative expression. Such opportunities are rarely provided in the usual "basic" curriculum, which usually takes place in authoritarian classrooms. These important nonacademic skills *can* be incorporated within the traditional curriculum, but teachers rarely receive the kind of professional development that makes them aware of the need for this different kind of teaching or the skills to incorporate them in their own classes. There never seems to be enough money for this kind of professional development.

But money always seems to be available for more coercive measures that serve the hidden goals of producing a subservient population. For example, in the January 2004 State of the Union speech, President Bush unveiled a $23 million plan for the drug testing of all students. Drug testing had already been introduced in some schools for students taking part in extracurricular activities and, despite challenges by privacy advocates, was upheld in 2002 by the Supreme Court. But this new policy would extend testing to *all* students.[2] The stated reason for this innovation was to discourage drug use and to identify users and help them break their habit. The president said, "The aim here is not to punish children but to send them this message: 'We love you, and we don't want to lose you.'"

But is this policy driven entirely by such noble sentiments? Surely there is a genuine concern about drug use among schoolchildren, and people can be excused for thinking that prevention of abuse is worth almost any price. But there is also reason to think that there are considerable negatives to such a policy. Opponents of testing have, for example, argued that the results of the tests might not be kept confidential and that students who test positive will end up being punished and publicly humiliated instead of being quietly helped.

But given the historical role of schools to condition students to their future role in society, another reason for this expanded drug-testing regimen might be to get people accustomed to their privacy being invaded while they are still young. It is not hard to imagine that children who are routinely subjected to drug testing and have this lack of trust and invasion of their privacy condoned by their parents and teachers (the main authority figures in their lives at that stage) are more likely to accept similar invasions of their privacy as adults. The same goes for their free-speech rights and other privacy rights. This is why parents and students have to guard their rights diligently. Protecting children from the temptation to use dangerous drugs or from violence is important, but we should not be quick to embrace solutions that also seek to condition children to unquestioningly accept authority and to be docile in the face of intrusions on their rights.[3]

The elite suburban and private schools function somewhat differently. While their students are subject to some of the same surveillance and intrusions on their privacy as their urban school counterparts, their landscaped grounds, open campus atmosphere, extracurricular options that provide leadership training, and less authoritarian teaching styles provide a less coercive atmosphere. But they too have to limit the aspirations of most of their students. They too have to institute a "cooling off" function so that many students will accept that they are to be satisfied with just middle-level jobs. In these jobs, they are the enforcers of rules and perpetuators of structures created by others. These students have to internalize the values on which these rules and structures are based so that they think of them as natural and just.

Thus an important, but hidden, function of schools is to be places where most students slowly get accustomed to the idea that they have to curb their ambitions, limit their dreams, and accept a reduced station in life. This lowering of expectations is achieved by experiences of repeated failure (in terms of academic tests) and acquiescence to authority. Students are also taught in mostly a didactic manner, giving them the impression that they are not authentic creators of knowledge but that they must be dependent on authority figures (political leaders, teachers, priests, and other "experts") to tell them what to believe and what to do.

In my conversations with people in walks of life similar to mine (people who have had a substantial amount of formal education and are in professional and managerial occupations that provide some measure of intellectual challenge and emotional satisfaction), they will readily agree that they themselves, as Aristotle asserted, enjoy learning for its own sake, that they flourish under conditions of autonomy, and that it is important to them that the work they do be interesting and challenging. They know that their own jobs provide them with considerable freedom in terms of what they do, how they do it, and even in choosing their hours of work. You cannot be successful at these kinds of jobs unless you have considerable self-regulating skills. For such people, it would be unthinkable to do the kinds of routine work for low remuneration done by the overwhelming majority of the population.

But what is interesting is that if you ask such people why only a few (like them) have access to these kinds of rewarding occupations, while most have to do routine work under close supervision with little autonomy, the answer you get is that most people do not to have the kinds of self-regulating qualities that are necessary for success in these professions and can only function in highly supervised tasks. There is the feeling that most people are only capable of doing boring and routine work, so they are well matched to their occupations. The trash collector does not have the qualities that would make him a successful college professor or engineer, and that is why he becomes a trash collector.

In other words, there is the implicit belief that the educational system has almost miraculously selected the right number and kinds of people to fill the kinds of jobs available. Seen in this light, the educational system has to be viewed as a remarkable success.

It never seems to strike such people that there is another interpretation for this seemingly serendipitous result, that the success of the educational system is not that it takes students with *preexisting* qualities and sorts them accurately into the right occupations, but that it actually *creates* the kinds of people that the world of work as currently constituted needs. After all, the present stratified society can only be sustained if there are a large number of people willing and able to work at low-paying, low-skilled jobs so that the rest can live much better lives doing challenging and creative work with much better rewards. In other words, the system is *designed* to take the entire set of eager and curious young children and, over time, create a stratified group of young adults, most of whom believe they are incapable of achieving anything meaningful in their work lives and look for emotional and intellectual satisfaction in recreation. It could be argued that the greatest "success" of the educational system is that it produces people who believe unquestioningly that the educational system is meritocratic and that their lowly station in life is natural and they should accept it.

We have to ask ourselves which model is more realistic: that the powerful in society leave it to chance that the educational system will produce the correct numbers of people to fit into these employment and economic niches, thus leaving their own positions secure, or that they deliberately set out to create an educational structure that will support such a system. But one does not have to depend on guesswork to answer that question. There is evidence that the correct answer is the second one.

The picture that has been painted of the role of the schools in our society might seem too dire and stark and controlling. It might even be viewed as being somewhat paranoid. But this thesis is not original at all. Serious observers of schools have long pointed out its social-conditioning purpose and the hidden and adverse aspects of the present schooling structure.[4] Perhaps one of the clearest, more recent descriptions of the hidden functions of school can be found in the book *Schooling in Capitalist America* by Samuel Bowles and Herbert Gintis, two professors of economics at the University of Massachusetts.[5] Although written in 1978, the book is still well worth reading by anyone who is interested in the way

schools have been used to achieve broader social goals. I believe that the
book's conclusions hold up well even after nearly three decades.

In the book, Bowles and Gintis carefully analyze the economic and
educational data and arrive at conclusions very similar to those articulated in this chapter. It is worthwhile to quote them at some length on
the similarity between school and work:

> [T]he educational system operates in this manner not so much through
> the conscious intentions of teachers and administrators in their day-to-day
> activities, but through a close correspondence between the social rela-
> tionships which govern personal interaction in the work place and the so-
> cial relationships of the educational system. Specifically, the relationships
> of authority and control between administrators and teachers, teachers
> and students, students and students, and students and their work replicate
> the hierarchical division of labor which dominates the work place. Power
> is organized along vertical lines of authority from administration to faculty
> to student body; students have a degree of control over their curriculum
> comparable to that of the worker over the content of his job. The motiva-
> tional system of the school, involving as it does grades and other external
> rewards and the threat of failure rather than the intrinsic social benefits of
> the process of education (learning) or its tangible outcome (knowledge),
> mirrors closely the role of wages and the specter of unemployment in the
> motivation of workers. The fragmented nature of jobs is reflected in the
> institutionalized and rarely constructive competition among students and
> in the specialization and compartmentalization of academic knowledge.
> Finally, the relationships of dominance and subordinancy in education dif-
> fer by level. The rule orientation of the high school reflects the close su-
> pervision of low-level workers; the internalization of norms and freedom
> from continual supervision in elite colleges reflect the social relationships
> of upper-level white-collar work. Most state universities and community
> colleges, which fall in between, conform to the behavioral requisites of
> low-level technical, service, and supervisory personnel.[6]

Bowles and Gintis also discuss the functions of the different school systems:

> These differences in the social relationships among and within schools, in
> part, reflect both the social backgrounds of the student body and their
> likely future economic positions. Thus blacks and other minorities are

concentrated in schools whose repressive, arbitrary, generally chaotic internal order, coercive authority structures, and minimal possibilities for advancement mirror the characteristics of inferior job situations. Similarly, predominantly working-class schools tend to emphasize behavioral control and rule-following, while schools in well-to-do suburbs employ relatively open systems that favor greater student participation, less direct supervision, more student electives, and, in general, a value system stressing internalized standards of control.[7]

Bowles and Gintis point out that influential liberal educators like John Dewey saw the purpose of school as seeking to fulfill three main goals[8]:

- Developmental: Achieve growth in the physical, cognitive, emotional, moral, and aesthetic qualities of children
- Egalitarian: Give everyone a chance to compete equally, by enabling education to overcome differentials in income and family background
- Integrative: Enable children to achieve a smooth transition into occupations and political and social life.

There can be no doubt as to the worth and appropriateness of the first two goals. The third one is also unimpeachable, provided that the "occupations and political and social life" that we prepare our students for are compatible with the first two goals. What happens though when this third goal, because of the nature of the occupations and social positions that the students are being prepared for in the modern corporate state, is in opposition to the other two? Therein lies the fundamental contradiction.

I have argued that the modern corporate state needs large numbers of people who are subservient to authority and who can be controlled by rewards and threats. It is this that makes for short-term efficiency in the marketplace. But in order to achieve that integrative goal, the developmental and egalitarian goals of education have to be sacrificed. Children have to be persuaded that school and work are not places where one achieves satisfaction. They have to seek meaning in life outside of work and school and must be persuaded that emotional and intellectual enjoyment in life must be sought with their families, friends, and the consumer culture, with its emphasis on sports and entertainment. Furthermore, children have to accept that inequality is a fact of life and, most importantly, that it is perfectly natural that many should be at the bottom of the ladder.

Hence Dewey's goals are mutually inconsistent for our society as currently structured. We cannot simultaneously achieve all three. Something has to yield, and given the way political power is wielded for the benefit of the corporate world, it should be no surprise that the last goal is the one that wins out at the expense of the other two.

Of course, one cannot completely get rid of the questioning impulse in people. People need to use their brains and to assert their autonomy and independence, at least in some spheres of their lives. Aristotle's saying, "All men by nature desire to know," with which this book began, applies to everyone, not just the elites. But most people tend to find outlets for their mental stimulation in sports and other elements of popular culture, while assuming that the world of government, business, public policy, finance, and international affairs is beyond them and should be left in the hands of experts. This ensures that major decisions are left in the hands of a few people, even though the consequences affect many, if not all.

Nowhere is the yearning for individuals to exercise the intellectual side of their personalities more apparent than in sports talk radio. Some people might feel that "sports talk radio" and "intellectual" do not belong in the same sentence. But listen to even a brief segment of these shows to see what I mean. Callers will devote enormous time and effort to analyzing sports matters. They will examine in careful detail the most arcane aspects of sports strategy and draw all kinds of inferences from the data. They are perfectly willing to challenge the expertise of professionals in the field and question the actions of players, coaches, and owners. They do not limit themselves just to the games either. They will also analyze the financial structure of sports teams and criticize management decisions and trades.

The quality of the arguments that are given in support of their positions can be quite variable, but that is not the issue here. The point is that the callers feel perfectly entitled to give their opinions and have clearly put quite a lot of thought into arriving at their often-intricate arguments. The amount of effort required is not that different or less than one might have to make to understand health-care policy, or tax policy, or foreign policy. Yet one rarely finds that level of passion and involvement for these latter topics among the general public, even though the personal relevance of these issues to the actual lives of real people is far greater than the issue of how to field a home team that might have a chance to win the Super Bowl.

Why is this? This comes back to our earlier analogy with games and puzzles. All of these require similar levels of effort and practice. But people *choose* one set of activities to devote their energies to and ignore others that may be more beneficial to their actual lives. Could it be that the reason people feel more at ease with seeming trivia is because such topics are not part of the school curriculum and so students have not been subjected to years of reading books by experts, listening to teachers, taking exams and doing poorly on them, and thus become reconciled to feeling that they know nothing about the subject? It is interesting to speculate on what might happen if sports were to become an academic subject and part of the regular curriculum, taught in a didactic fashion with high-pressure tests that require the memorization of arcane information such as individual batting averages. Would the next generation of students become too intimidated by the subject to voice any authentic opinions? Is this the way to kill off sports talk radio?

This line of speculation may seem far-fetched, but it is worthwhile to reflect a little on educational history and see what insights can be gleaned from it. Currently, there is widespread concern about the low levels of reading skills among children, and there are many efforts to raise reading scores. But John Taylor Gatto, in his book *The Underground History of American Education*,[9] points out that at the time of the American Revolution, before mandatory mass schooling came into being, there was almost universal literacy among the white public. This was because people were learning to read spontaneously. And they were not learning to read using specialized "Dick and Jane and Spot" type readers, which require low-level vocabulary and grammar. They were reading books and political pamphlets and newspapers written for adults. People were learning to read because they had something worth reading, and learning that skill gave them greater power and control over their lives. It is a bitter irony that 200 years later, with all children going to school and being taught by trained, highly educated professionals, reading skills have declined so much that many children now have to be coaxed to learn to read.

A situation analogous to reading has arisen in this day. We all know that children who have access to computers are highly adept at using them and at navigating the Internet. They learn to do so on their own and by sharing information with their peers and are far more at ease with this technology than even their parents and teachers. They acquire these skills spontaneously, just like reading was acquired 200 years ago. And the reasons are the same. The students can explore on their own, and as they do so, they pick up whatever knowledge and skills they need. The Internet also offers them benefits that they can immediately enjoy. Learning to use it is its own reward. Parents do not have to bribe their children to surf the Web. Instead, children have to be pried away from their computers and limitations placed on their use.

But already we see efforts to introduce computers and the Internet into the formal curriculum. It is only a matter of time before computing and Web surfing become part of the daily school routine. If the pattern outlined above holds true and these topics are taught in the same mind-numbing way that much of, say, mathematics and science is currently taught, then maybe in a few generations children will have to be coaxed to use computers as well.

Gatto points out that much of the regimented schooling we see today arose from fears (around the birth of the twentieth century) that the growth of widespread, spontaneous, but unregulated education was resulting in a population that was asking too many inconvenient questions and was leading to social unrest as people started demanding what they felt was rightfully theirs. While unrest could be temporarily suppressed with force using the police and the private Pinkerton security agency, such a solution was messy and unstable. The educational system was perceived as being able to provide an invisible means of control, provided it was properly designed and implemented.

In his book, Gatto unearths a set of revealing quotes from influential policymakers who deliberately set out to create the system that would produce large numbers of students who enter the workplace already defeated. The reasons for doing so were stated quite clearly. In 1872, the U.S. Bureau of Education published a *Circular for Information* expressing concern that "'inculcating knowledge' teaches workers to be able to 'perceive and calculate the grievances,' thus making them 'more redoubtable foes' in labor struggles." This was followed in 1888 by a report of the Senate Committee on Education, which stated, "We believe that education is one of the principal causes of discontent of late years manifesting itself among the laboring classes."[10]

The response to this challenge to the interests of the propertied classes was to push for an educational system that would pacify the public and make them accept their assigned status. The famous philosopher and educator John Dewey articulated the view that education should serve the needs of society when he wrote in 1897, "Every teacher should realize he is a social servant set apart for the maintenance of the proper social order and the securing of the right social growth."[11]

Elwood Cubberly, dean of education at Stanford University and another highly influential educational policymaker, wrote in his 1905 dissertation for Columbia Teachers College that in the future schools should be factories "in which raw products, children, are to be shaped and formed into finished products . . . manufactured like nails, and the specifications for manufacturing will come from government and industry."[12]

In 1912, the Rockefeller Foundation–backed General Education Board—which funded the creation of numerous public schools—issued a statement that read in part:

In our dreams . . . people yield themselves with perfect docility to our molding hands. The present educational conventions [intellectual and character education] fade from our minds, and unhampered by tradition we work our own good will upon a grateful and responsive folk. We shall not try to make these people or any of their children into philosophers or men of learning or men of science. We have not to raise up from among them authors, educators, poets or men of letters. We shall not search for embryo great artists, painters, musicians, nor lawyers, doctors, preachers, politicians, statesmen, of whom we have ample supply. The task we set before ourselves is very simple. . . . We will organize children . . . and teach them to do in a perfect way the things their fathers and mothers are doing in an imperfect way.[13]

It is hard to fully comprehend the calm way in which this heartless and cruel statement callously consigns most children to a deliberate intellectual death.

The logical end point of this line of thinking was quite clear. It was necessary to create an educational system that produced a large number of passive and uncritical people who would basically do as they were told. What is quite surprising (at least to present-day ears) is the brazenness with which these highly antiegalitarian ideas were expressed. Proposals that would (and should) be considered by humane people as outrageous and unjust social engineering are expressed matter-of-factly by influential people. President Woodrow Wilson said in a speech to businessmen, "We want one class to have a liberal education. We want another class, a very much larger class of necessity, to forego the privilege of a liberal education and fit themselves to perform specific difficult manual tasks."[14]

And William Torrey Harris, U.S. Commissioner of Education from 1889 to 1906, wrote in his *The Philosophy of Education*, "Ninety-nine [students] out of a hundred are automata, careful to walk in prescribed paths, careful to follow the prescribed custom. *This is not an accident but the result of substantial education*, which, scientifically defined, is the subsumption of the individual."[15] (emphasis added)

The most extreme form of this philosophy led to classrooms that prepared children for a lifetime of assembly-line work where people were expected to do repetitive tasks mindlessly. The traditional classroom where students sat in orderly rows and did not talk or otherwise interact with one another but looked straight at the teacher and followed instructions that were internalized by repeated drilling was an ideal preparation for such a life. The mind-numbing, repetitive nature of this existence was brutally captured by Charlie Chaplin in his film *Modern Times*.

Fortunately we have moved away (at least in official statements, if not in practice) from such a bleak vision of education, although it surprises me that many well-meaning people still look back on those classrooms as the golden years of education. The ideas of cooperative learning, active and interactive classrooms, and constructivist models of learning have all led to more relaxed classrooms where there is a chance that students can recapture the joys of learning. It would be nice to think that the changes that have occurred are due entirely to a more enlightened view of education and a more humane approach toward schoolchildren. But it surely cannot be a coincidence that some of these changes are concurrent with the decline of manufacturing and the assembly-line model of production in the United States. The current rise of the service-sector economy requires a different set of educational and social skills than in the past, although the business ideal of having a large pool of docile workers willing to work for minimal wages still remains.

As I have mentioned before, the thesis that in order to understand the structure of the educational system, we need to understand the needs of the economy is hardly new. A little thought will convince anyone that it can hardly be otherwise. Is it really conceivable that the educational system can evolve independently of the needs of the workplace? Most people will accept that such a link must exist but will think the link is more benign than portrayed in this book.

We have to be able to see beyond the lip service to education often provided by business leaders and their political allies. These people are fond of making pronouncements about how they would like the educational system to provide highly skilled workers who can think critically, manage complex tasks, and work well in teams. What is left unsaid is that they also want such workers to work for minimum wage or less, without adequate health and retirement benefits, and to be docile and obedient, to not agitate for better conditions, to not feel a sense of solidarity with their fellow workers or the broad mass of people, and to be accepting of summary firing and layoffs as part of the legitimate needs of business and the cost of enabling capital to move freely from place to place and even to other countries.

But educators do not have to, and should not, accept those goals. We are *teachers*, inheritors of a noble and high calling, not the training and enforcement arm of the modern corporate state. We should be maximizing the learning potential and skills of students, not teaching them to aim low, to conform, to think of themselves as capable of only low-level tasks. So what should we do? If, as I assert, we cannot in the current economic structure teach to simultaneously meet all three of Dewey's developmental, egalitarian, and integrative goals, which ones should we be aiming for? Clearly, my preference is that we should be aiming for the first two. What we should be also trying to achieve simultaneously is the creation of a society where the third goal would not be, as it is now, in conflict with the other two, but would conform to it. In other words, we should seek a society that can absorb the people who have fully developed their developmental and egalitarian qualities, instead of creating people to fit into a society that does not want or need large numbers of people with highly developed physical, cognitive, emotional, moral, and aesthetic qualities, and who also have egalitarian goals.

The reader might be tempted to dismiss the possibility of creating such an enlightened educational system as hopelessly idealistic and unattainable. But why is it that we react in this pessimistic manner to something that should be so desirable? Bowles and Gintis say that this is due to our being presented with analyses of modern political, social, and economic life that are based on faulty premises. "[W]e have shown that the cynicism bred by modern mainstream economics, sociology, and political science is based on a series of myths: that hierarchical authority is necessitated by modern technology; that inequality is due to unequal abilities; that capitalism is already meritocratic; and that the existing situation corresponds to people's needs and is the product of their wills."[16]

Working toward the creation of a more humane and enlightened society is a political act, and it would be idle of me to pretend that it does not have serious consequences. It might be feared that not producing the kinds of workers that businesses currently require might result in economic disruptions and to businesses' outsourcing some jobs overseas. But that form of job migration is already happening, and the nature of the outsourced jobs are already increasing from the unskilled and semiskilled jobs that were traditionally farmed out to poorer countries, to more skilled jobs in the technology and technical services industries. Already, highly skilled jobs that can be done over the Internet (such as software development, tax preparation, telecommunication, telephone help-desk services, and radiological diagnostics) are going overseas.

Whatever the economic impact, teaching our students in such a manner that the natural desire to learn is enhanced and built upon is the only *ethical* option that we as teachers have, and we cannot ignore that obligation. Looking at the field of medical care, we rightly condemn the actions of those physicians who deny proper health care to patients in order to serve the needs of health insurance companies or who have harmed people and animals by experimenting on them unethically in the service of a purportedly greater social good. The medical profession has guidelines that prohibit doing harm to individuals. Most beginning physicians as they enter their profession take a form of the Hippocratic

Oath, which serves to remind them that their fundamental responsibility is to serve the needs of patients and their families.

Teachers do not have a formal ethical code like physicians. Perhaps it is time to adopt one. Perhaps we teachers should also take an oath that reminds us that our primary responsibility is to the long-term well-being of our students, not to serve the goals of social engineers or employers' needs or political agendas. I propose a four-point Aristotelian Oath that could be the starting point for discussion.

The first point would state:

- We pledge, as teachers, to have as our fundamental goal in teaching any subject, to create in our students a love of learning for its own sake.

For the other three points, we could reformulate Dewey's three goals in a slightly different way. The first two of Dewey's goals (the developmental and egalitarian) could be largely unchanged[17]:

- We pledge to work toward growth in the physical, cognitive, emotional, moral, and aesthetic qualities of children.
- We pledge to give everyone a chance to compete equally, by enabling education to overcome differentials in income and family background.

But for the fourth point, the integrative goal will need to be modified[18]:

- We pledge to work with our students to create a society where children nurtured by the first three goals can achieve a smooth transition into compatible occupations and political and social life, so that they may lead fulfilling lives.

Of course, adopting a teacher's Aristotelian Oath is not going to solve the problems of education or close the achievement gap any more than taking the Hippocratic Oath solves all the problems confronting the world of health care. What are needed to achieve those goals are the long-term, ongoing, painstaking efforts outlined in the previous chapters. But such an oath, hanging on our walls, might continually remind us of our primary duty as teachers, that our responsibility is to our students, to enable them to realize their full potential. Society has to adapt itself to the needs of such students. It is not our role to produce students to fit into whatever slots society dictates.

Is this goal too ambitious? Perhaps, but as teachers, we really have no other ethical choice. Trust is an important part of any learning–teaching relationship. Our students put their trust in us to do what is best for *them*. We must not betray that trust.

NOTES

1. Matt Groening, *School Is Hell* (New York: Pantheon Books, 1987).

2. Lara Jakes Jordan, Associated Press, "Concerns Simmer as Government Seeks to Expand Student Drug Testing," *Plain Dealer*, 1 February 2004, A20.

3. The assault on privacy can be seen in many different venues. Since the attacks on the World Trade Center on September 11, 2001, there has been a massive assault on people's privacy, under the umbrella of fighting terrorism. Increasingly intrusive checking at airports and monitoring of what people view and read has now been made legal under the provisions of the USA PATRIOT act. Despite the constant fearmongering, there has still been some resistance to these moves against individual liberties. Librarians, not normally viewed as militant activists, have been up in arms against laws that require them to secretly turn over library-patron records to government investigators. These laws prevent library staffers from mentioning that they have done so to anyone, including their colleagues, their bosses, or even the library patron whose reading and viewing habits are being requested.

4. Ivan Illich, *Deschooling Society* (New York: Harper Collins, 1983); Paulo Freire, *Pedagogy of the Oppressed* (New York: Continuum, 2000).

5. Samuel Bowles and Herbert Gintis, *Schooling in Capitalist America* (New York: Basic Books, 1976).

6. Bowles and Gintis, *Schooling in Capitalist America*, 11.

7. Bowles and Gintis, *Schooling in Capitalist America*, 132.

8. Bowles and Gintis, *Schooling in Capitalist America*, 21. Bowles and Gintis formulate these goals based on John Dewey, *Democracy and Education* (New York: The Free Press, 1916).

9. John Taylor Gatto, *The Underground History of American Education* (New York: The Oxford Village Press, 2003).

10. Gatto, *The Underground History of American Education*, 153.

11. Gatto, *The Underground History of American Education*, xxvii.

12. Gatto, *The Underground History of American Education*, footnote to page 39 in online version of the book, omitted in printed version.

13. Gatto, *The Underground History of American Education*, 45.

14. Gatto, *The Underground History of American Education*, 38.

15. Gatto, *The Underground History of American Education*, 105.

16. Bowles and Gintis, *Schooling in Capitalist America*, 269.

17. Bowles and Gintis, *Schooling in Capitalist America*, 21.

18. Bowles and Gintis, *Schooling in Capitalist America*, 21.

INDEX

academic resources, 63, 83

accountability, 84, 86, 104, 139, 141, 147, 148

active learning, 6, 100, 119, 131, 137, 146, 148, 176

Adelman, Clifford, 63, 65, 82–83, 95

advanced placement (AP), 12, 16, 23, 42, 109–10, 131, 145

affirmative action, 29, 37–38, 49, 153

alignment, 122–23, 141

Aristotle, 9, 11, 14, 152, 168, 172, 179

Arons, Arnold, 143–44, 155–57

Aronson, Joshua, 73, 79

The Art of Changing the Brain, 2, 8, 106, 133

assessments, 35, 120–24, 127, 140–43

authoritarian, 7, 20, 122, 127–28, 137, 166–67

Baldwin, James, 31, 44

basic skills, 86, 91–92

The Bell Curve, 43, 45, 48, 50, 55, 57

benchmarks, 87, 121, 132, 140

Benezet, Louis, 115–16, 134

Berliner, David, 22–23, 28

bias, 2, 19, 20, 34, 47, 69, 142–43

Biddle, Bruce, 22–23, 28

Biggs, John, 119–20, 131, 134

Binet, Alfred, 52

The Black Commentator, 32, 44

The Black–White Test Score Gap, 44, 65, 78–79, 133–34, 157

Bowles, Samuel, 169–71, 178, 180–81

Bracey, Gerald, 22–23, 28, 57

bribes, 9, 14, 17

canaries in the mine, 26

Chickering, Arthur, 119

class sizes, 34–35, 70

Cleveland, 15–17, 33, 40–41, 98, 111, 146

constructivism, 100, 107, 176

ABOUT THE AUTHOR

Mano Singham is director of Case Western Reserve University's University Center for Innovation in Teaching and Education (UCITE) and adjunct associate professor of physics. He obtained his B.Sc. from the University of Colombo in Sri Lanka and his M.S. and Ph.D. degrees in theoretical nuclear physics from the University of Pittsburgh. Before coming to Case in 1989, he taught and carried out research at the University of Rochester, Los Alamos National Laboratory, Drexel University, University of Pittsburgh, and the University of Colombo.

Singham has researched and conducted seminars and workshops for university faculty on teaching and learning. He has conducted workshops around the country on active-learning methods for science teachers at precollege and college levels and run summer and academic year programs for K–12 science teachers. He also worked for five years as scientist–educator for Project Discovery, one of the National Science Foundations's Statewide Systemic Initiatives to improve K–12 science education. He has also conducted cognitive coaching seminars for school administrators.

Singham is a fellow of the American Physical Society. In 2001 he won Case Western Reserve University's Carl F. Wittke award for distinguished undergraduate teaching and has received numerous other awards for teaching and service to education. He has written articles and given invited talks on "The Achievement Gap in Science and Mathematics Education," "Active Learning," and "Science and Religion" at professional meetings of scientists and educators. His recent research interests are in the fields of education, theories of knowledge, and physics and philosophy. His first book, *The Quest for Truth: Scientific Progress and Religious Beliefs*, was published by Phi Delta Kappan Educational Foundation in November 2000.